AFGHANI AND 'ABDUH

AFGHANI AND 'ABDUH

AN ESSAY ON RELIGIOUS UNBELIEF
AND POLITICAL ACTIVISM IN
MODERN ISLAM

ELIE KEDOURIE

FRANK CASS
LONDON · PORTLAND, OR.

Published in 1997 by
FRANK CASS & CO. LTD.
Newbury House, 900 Eastern Avenue
London, IG2 7HH

and c/o ISBS, 5804 N.E. Hassalo Street
Portland, Oregon, 97213-3644

First Published 1966
Reprinted 1997

Transferred to Digital Printing 2005

Copyright © 1966 Elie Kedourie
Foreword copyright © 1997 Sylvia Kedourie

British Library Cataloguing in Publication Data:

A catalogue record for this book is available
from the British Library

ISBN 0-7146-1989-2 (cloth)
ISBN 0-7146-4355-6 (paper)

Library of Congress Cataloging-in-Publication Data:

A catalog record for this book is available
from the Library of Congress

All rights reserved. No part of this publication may be reproduced
in any form or by any means, electronic, mechanical, photocopying,
recording or otherwise, without the prior permission of
Frank Cass and Company Limited.

CONTENTS

Preface ... vii

1997 Foreword by Sylvia Kedourie ... ix

AFGHANI AND 'ABDUH ... 1

APPENDICES:

    I. 'Abduh's Letter to Afghani, Beirut, 1883 ... 66

   II. Afghani's Articles in *L'Intransigeant*, Paris, 1883 ... 70

  III. Afghani's Letter to the British Ambassador, Constantinople, 1895 ... 87

Notes ... 89

PREFACE

For over half a century Jamal al-Din al-Afghani and his follower Muhammad 'Abduh have been accepted entirely at their own valuation. The prevalent account of their career, for which they themselves are largely responsible, diligently advertised by their numerous and faithful disciples, exhibits them as devoted and pious reformers of Islam. This picture turns out on closer examination to have little to do with the reality. But if the actual beliefs and activities of Afghani and 'Abduh are not as edifying as has been generally thought, yet as will be seen from these pages, they are perhaps more curious and significant than the hagiographers have made out.

Two students of Middle Eastern history, Miss Sylvia G. Haim and Mrs. Nikki R. Keddie, in the course of examining Arab and Persian nationalism respectively were led independently of each other to make some remarks on Afghani which aroused in me curiosity and puzzlement and led me to the present investigation. The work of both of them appeared in 1962. In 1963, most opportunely, there was published in Teheran a collection of documents belonging to Afghani which had lain undisturbed since his expulsion from Persia in 1891. These documents and the other sources examined here shed a peculiar light on the origins of so-called reformism in contemporary Islam. Suddenly, therefore, in the space of some two years, the received version of Afghani's and 'Abduh's history has been damaged seemingly beyond repair. The episode constitutes a pleasing illustration of the fortuitous and unpredictable character of historiographical progress.

Parts of this Essay have appeared in *Orient* (Paris) and *Middle Eastern Studies* (London).

August, 1965

E. K.

FOREWORD

This book, completed in August 1965, sold out soon after its publication in 1966. I have decided to allow its republication as the subject matter is even more relevant today than at the time of publication – a time when Islam had not yet come so much to the fore. Arab nationalism, seemingly in its apogee, and claiming to be above religious and sectarian divides, ruled the day.

At the turn of the century, however, people were looking for enlightened reformers who would be able to bridge the cultural divide between East and West, and whose Koranic interpretations would accommodate the necessary change to help the East attain the same degree of progress which the West enjoyed. Who better than Muhammad 'Abduh, Grand Mufti of Egypt could be counted as such? And 'Abduh acknowledged a great debt to Jamal al-Din al-Afghani.

Now that Arab nationalism has receded, extreme forms of Islam are striving to gain the upper hand on more than one front. The so-called 'fundamentalists' are fighting not only foreign infiltration and foreign powers, but they are also fighting traditional and established forms of Islam. People, many of whom are undoubtedly devout Muslims, will again be looking to find Islamic arguments to turn the tide of zealotry which threatens to engulf their lives. What better models and teachers to turn to than the enlightened reformers? And 'Abduh, Grand Mufti of Egypt, gave certainly enlightened interpretations of Islam. But is this the whole story, or is there another side to the coin?

In this classic study, Elie Kedourie re-examines the validity of Afghani's and 'Abduh's reputations as enlightened reformers. Basing his work on newly published documentary evidence and other sources, he reaches conclusions far removed from the reputations which had been posthumously nurtured.

Sylvia Kedourie

January, 1997

Iago: Heaven is my judge, not I for love and duty,
But seeming so, for my peculiar end:
For when my outward action doth demonstrate
The native act, and figure of my heart
In complement extern, 'tis not long after
But I will wear my heart upon my sleeve
For daws to peck at; I am not what I am.

Othello, Act I, scene 1.

What the subject is, is the series of his actions.

Hegel

AFGHANI AND 'ABDUH

Sayyid Jamal al-Din al-Afghani, and his best known disciple Shaikh Muhammad 'Abduh, enjoy today, East and West, a high reputation as defenders and reformers of modern Islam. The first is known in Arabic literature as *hakim al-sharq*, the Sage of the East, while the second is scarcely less well known as the Teacher and the Guide—*al-ustadh al-imam*—titles bestowed upon him by his follower and biographer, Rashid Rida. Leaving aside Oriental literature for the moment who, among western writers, it may be asked, originated the reputation which Afghani and 'Abduh now enjoy? The answer is that Afghani figures among the heroes of Professor Edward G. Browne's *Persian Revolution* which was published in 1910; that he and more particularly 'Abduh, cut a considerable figure in the voluminous diaries which Wilfrid Scawen Blunt began publishing in the first decade of the twentieth century, in order to denounce the oppressions of the British Government and promote the cause of its victims; and finally that 'Abduh is sympathetically, if ambiguously, presented in Lord Cromer's *Modern Egypt*, which was published in 1908. That these two figures should be presented under such auspices as *Islamic* reformers must give us pause: Blunt's sympathy with 'Urabi's movement, in which 'Abduh was involved, is well-known, whilst it is notorious that Professor Browne was no mere academic historian, but rather a deeply committed partisan of Persian nationalism—which Afghani was thought to have promoted; he was indeed a believer in the beneficence of any nationalism on the ground that "in this world diversity, not uniformity, is the higher law and the more desirable state";[1] as for Cromer, he approved of 'Abduh because he thought that his influence made for a less rigid Islam, one more open to wholesome European influence, and because the Mufti of Egypt was a welcome change from what he considered to be the usual run of obscurantist Muslim divine; it may indeed have been a recommendation in Cromer's eyes that "my friend Abduh" as he put it, "was in reality an agnostic";[2] more pertinent than all this perhaps—though Cromer does not discuss it—was the fact that in his last years of respectability and eminence Shaikh Muhammad 'Abduh was in opposition to Abbas Hilmi and hence an ally in Cromer's unremitting battle against the Khedive.

It is worth dwelling on this last point. 'Abduh and Afghani were all through their lives primarily men of action, involved in complicated and obscure transactions. To understand what they were, and what they stood for, we must have knowledge of their activities; and yet it is by their overt professions and aspirations, by what they said and not by what they did that we are mostly invited to judge them; and so we see writers expending their ingenuity in an attempt to find a system in Afghani's involved and mediocre journalism, or to discover reasons why 'Abduh's superficial theology should be admired. This tendency to assume that speech is a pointer to action is understandable, since in the modern West, with its open and vigorous public life, there is usually some kind of connexion between what is said and what is done. But when dealing with men like Afghani and 'Abduh who had to live and act under oriental despotisms, had we not better assume that what is done has no necessary connection with what is said, and that what is said in public, may be quite different from what is believed in private?

Doubts have recently been cast on the account traditionally given of 'Abduh's and Afghani's teachings and activities. In a most original paper on "Religion and Irreligion in early Iranian Nationalism",³ Professor Nikki R. Keddie has argued that Afghani wished to use Islam for political purposes. The same view is taken by Sylvia G. Haim in the introduction to her *Arab Nationalism: an Anthology*,⁴ who makes the point that Afghani's real belief was that all religions, Islam included, were equally bad. She agrees with Professor Keddie that Afghani had an esoteric as well as an exoteric doctrine and says that his bent was "utilitarian, sceptical and activist"; she states that "he was the very type of revolutionary conspirator and activist so well known in Europe in modern times" and that it is "only his remoteness from the main stream of European history, together with his clerical garb, his reputation as a religious thinker ... and the scant and contradictory nature of the facts of his life, that may have obscured the true character of the man and the real nature and portent of his activities". Of 'Abduh, Miss Haim writes that as a consequence of his views Islam "ceases to be properly a religion and is transformed into a system of ethics or rules for successful conduct in this life" and that his teaching, meliorist and progressive, would have been dismissed "with contempt and hostility" by orthodox, traditional Islam.⁵ A careful examination of the evidence available tends to confirm and amplify such conclusions.

To understand the role and significance of Afghani and 'Abduh, it is necessary to bear in mind that their reputation and influence is to a large extent posthumous, the work of disciples, or else of academic writers and publicists eager to discover trends and precursors, and hence perhaps tending, like the disciples but from other motives, to magnify the importance of their subjects. Blunt, Browne and Cromer all wrote after the death both of Afghani and 'Abduh; 'Abduh's ideas did not become known in the West to any great extent until his theological treatise, *Risalat al-Tauhid* was published in a French translation, with a long introduction by B. Michel and Moustapha Abdel Razik in 1925, and until C. C. Adams published in 1933 his substantial and widely-read *Islam and Modernism in Egypt*.⁶ This observation is true not only of 'Abduh and Afghani but of many other figures who have in due course and after many years been discovered as harbingers and precursors. The general point may be illustrated by the case of Abd al-Rahman al-Kawakibi, a contemporary of both 'Abduh and Afghani, who was presented in George Antonius' *Arab*

Awakening as a significant figure in the genesis of Arab nationalism. That such a judgement made people eager to read Kawakibi, and thus in fact enhanced his reputation, does not make it any the less both subjective and retrospective. In his lifetime Kawakibi, as the evidence shows,[7] was an obscure scribbler and political agent to whom nobody paid much attention: "He was not known in his city of Aleppo" writes Shaikh Abd al-Qadir al-Maghribi, "as he is known in Cairo, Damascus and elsewhere. I myself have asked—as others have too—many inhabitants of Aleppo concerning his early years and his reputation for goodness among them. To start with, they used to pretend not to have heard of him, but after further exhaustive description, they would say that he was nothing out of the ordinary, that he was a nondescript character, who has left nothing to remember him by. Others went even so far as to accuse him of what it is unlikely that he should have been or done".[8] Afghani and 'Abduh were of course never as obscure as Kawakibi. They had travelled, lived and been politically active in Europe; and 'Abduh towards the end of his life was Mufti of Egypt. But their actual activities and real beliefs have remained quite unknown. The only version of their history which has obtained currency is one which they themselves inspired, and which their followers assiduously spread. It is this version which one sees uniformly presented in Orientalist literature, from which one representative quotation will suffice. "It was an essential element in his thought", writes Gibb of Afghani in a book published in 1947, "that the Muslim peoples should purify themselves from religious errors and compromises, that Muslim scholars should be abreast of modern currents of thought, and that the Muslim state should stand out as the political expression and vehicle of sound Koranic orthodoxy."[9] Afghani would no doubt have been much gratified to see that half a century after his death, his pretentions to "sound Koranic orthodoxy" were still being unquestioningly accepted.

During his lifetime, Afghani attracted the attention not so much of thinkers and statesmen, as, intermittently, that of security and intelligence departments whose business it was to follow the activities of subversives and agitators. When the Khedive Taufiq expelled him from Egypt in 1879, *The Times*, reporting the incident, described him as a "certain Gamad-ed-Din, an Afghan of doubtful antecedents"[10] and obviously knew little more about him. Seven years later exact knowledge about him had increased so little that we find Sir Evelyn Baring informing London in

Afghani and 'Abduh 5

a despatch that he had learnt from an Indian acquaintance that "the well-known Gellal-Eddin" had left Paris for Petersburg.[11] To Baring "Gellal-Eddin" would be well-known as the editor of a subversive print, published in Paris, *al-Urwa al-wuthqa*, which the authorities in India and Egypt were at pains to deny entry to their territories. But there is weightier evidence than a mere mistake in identification. In 1895 Afghani, then at Istanbul, some two years before his death finding himself in Sultan Abdul Hamid's bad books, and threatened with extradition to Persia where he was wanted for subversion, applied to the British Ambassador for protection as an Afghan subject. Sir Philip Currie who, a few years before, had had occasion, when at the Foreign Office, to become acquainted with Afghani's record, refused the request. Thereupon, Afghani, leaving the Embassy, went to the Consulate where he had no difficulty in having issued to him a pass, enabling him to leave Ottoman territory, in the quality of a "gentleman resident at Cabul"![12] The manoeuvre is pretty, but would have surely failed had Afghani been at all widely known. In fact, the *dossier* on Afghani which the Foreign Office compiled—now classified as F.O. 60/594—to which Professor Keddie was the first to draw attention—was put together as a result of Afghani's application, in order to determine the legal issue whether or not this man was entitled to claim Her Majesty's protection.

Afghani's eminence, then, was very much a posthumous affair, and the same is true, though not to the same extent, of 'Abduh. For the greater part of his life, he was a middling official in the Egyptian public service. In 1882, he had been involved in 'Urabi's movement and suffered, in consequence, the penalty of exile for some six years. He returned to Egypt in 1889, at a time when the British authorities began to feel that their position was somewhat more secure, and Baring could think it judicious and profitable to conciliate and attach to the British connexion former opponents and enemies. It was not until 1899, however, only six years before his death, that 'Abduh was appointed Mufti of Egypt and attained, in consequence, a position of some power and much influence. This position he achieved not only by virtue of his office, of his intellectual ability and of his acquaintance with European ideas—which were greater than those of most contemporary divines—but also because he was a supporter of Cromer, whom Cromer therefore in turn supported.

The posthumous renown of Afghani and 'Abduh impedes a proper understanding of their actual role and activities, since it constitutes a standing temptation to assume that they were as eminent during their lifetime as they became after their death. Their actual obscurity during much of their lives adds to the difficulty of piecing their history together, since they were not important enough for a continuous, systematic record of their activities to be kept and preserved; rather do we have to depend on scattered, fragmentary references in the writings of contemporaries, or in the official archives whenever governments had to take notice of Afghani, 'Abduh and their activities; and finally we must depend on posthumous compilations and biographies, and therefore on what the writers of such works thought interesting and advisable to preserve. In this last category, by far the most important work is Rashid Rida's *Tarikh al-ustadh al-imam*, the first volume of which, published in 1931, is a very long, not to say prolix, biography of 'Abduh, containing at its beginning a useful collection of biographical notices on Afghani by different hands. This massive and detailed work has, however, to be used with some caution since both 'Abduh and Rashid Rida, as will appear, practised economy of truth. Indeed Rashid Rida himself says of 'Abduh that "he was not used to divulge his thoughts without precautions except to a few individuals. Of some of his opinions he used to tell me that they were not to be written down or mentioned to anyone"; again, discussing 'Abduh's view of the Shi'ites, Rashid Rida wrote:

> "He mentioned to me what he never allowed me to report in his lifetime, and what I deem it wiser not to divulge after his death. I will only say that his judgment on them was harsher than that of *shaikh al-islam*, Ibn Taymiyya."[13]

This reticence, we observe, was being practised twenty-six years after 'Abduh's death. It is entirely characteristic of Rashid Rida; anybody who has had occasion to consult his periodical *al-Manar* concerning the political transactions in which he was involved will agree that he is, in many places, impenetrably discreet;[14] indeed, he himself said to George Antonius who was seeking information about Kawakibi: "not everything which is known can be spoken of, and not everything which is spoken can be written".[15]

Of Afghani's earliest years, from 1838 when he was born until 1871 when he appears in Egypt, little is known. He asserted that he was an Afghan, but there is little doubt now that he was by origin a Persian and a Shi'ite.* He also claimed that in the 1860s he took a prominent part in Afghan politics. In fact, as Professor Keddie establishes,[16] Afghani had some part to play in the troubled politics of Afghanistan during that period, but most probably as a Russian agent. Afghani then appears in 1870 in Istanbul, where he was employed in the Board of Education. A university on Western lines had just been established, and a series of public lectures was organized by its Director, who asked for volunteers to speak on various sciences. Afghani delivered a lecture on crafts in the body politic which aroused the displeasure of the religious authorities by its heterodox opinions, which caused him to be expelled from Istanbul, whence he went to Egypt.[17] It is interesting to note in passing that the particular point on which Afghani's critics in Istanbul fastened was that he likened Muhammad's prophetic office to any other vocation or profession necessary to the body politic.[18] We may remember here Dr. Abd al-Rahman Badawi's acute observation that irreligion in Islam more often takes the form of an attack on the prophetic office than on the Godhead.[19]

In his biographical notice 'Abduh states that Afghani originally came to Egypt only as a tourist and that he had no intention of remaining until the minister Mustafa Riad Pasha (1834-1911) persuaded him to stay. We do not know what attracted Riad to Afghani whom, according to Adib Ishaq, he had met in Istanbul,[20] but as we are told by a friend of Adib Ishaq's and a member of Afghani's circle in Cairo from 1878, Riad allowed Afghani to teach in al-Azhar, appointing to him a salary and lodgings within the mosque.[21] 'Abduh's later contention, as recorded by Rashid Rida, "that they appointed a salary of 1,000 Egyptian piastres a month for him as a gratuity and not for work he was required to do"[22] seems a deliberate attempt to magnify Afghani's

* Afghani did, on occasion, when it suited him, claim that he was a Shi'ite divine; see his article in the *Contemporary Review*, LXI, 1892, "The Reign of Terror in Persia"; he writes, p. 239, "My title, 'Son of the Prophet', may serve to signify to all Europeans that I am known and well accredited throughout the Dominions of the Shah, recognised in my high religious dignity by the Shah himself and all his Ministers and Ambassadors and upholders of our holy religion, and accepted as one of the chief teachers of the people." Ahmed Agayof has stated that Afghani personally told him that he was born near Hamadan and belonged to an Azari Turkish family from Maraghah; see Sharif al-Mujahid, *Jamal al-Din al-Afghani* . . . , M.A. thesis, 1954 McGill University, p. 37. In a forthcoming biography of Afghani, Professor Keddie conclusively establishes Afghani's Persian origin and upbringing.

position in 1871, by pretending that his eminence was such, even then, as to qualify him for an unconditional pension from the Egyptian Government. 'Anhuri's account is more convincing. He says that Riad cautioned Afghani to keep to the teachings of the *Shari'a* and of religion, that Afghani was diligent in this course for a while, praying and fasting regularly, until he formed a following drawn from those Azhar students who had "a lively intelligence and a penetrating mind". He then, says 'Anhuri, left his lodgings at al-Azhar and took a house in the Jewish quarter which became the meeting-place of his followers and those who depended on him.[23]

It seems then, to be a fact, the importance of which will appear presently, that he was the retainer and client of Riad Pasha. The fact must have been reasonably well-known, and we catch an echo of it—albeit a distorted one—in a memorandum on Afghani written in 1896 by the General Superintendent of the Thagi and Dakaiti Department at Calcutta in which it is stated that Afghani's journalistic activities in Paris in 1884 were financed by "Riaz Pasha and his many other friends in Egypt".[24] It is unlikely that Riad Pasha should have been financing revolutionary attacks on the Khedive's regime in 1884, but the earlier connexion was no doubt the basis of the Indian police's mistake.

From 1871 to 1878 little is heard of Afghani, but we know that in those years he gathered together a following which enabled him in 1878 and 1879 to take some part in the disturbed politics of Egypt in the last year of Isma'il's reign. One of those who attached themselves to him was Muhammad 'Abduh. Born in 1849, he was since 1866 a student at al-Azhar and, under the influence of a relative, a seeker after mystical experience. When 'Abduh met Afghani he was some twenty-two years old, an ardent young man going through a crucial phase in his spiritual life, and this no doubt made him impressionable; but Afghani must have had a powerful magnetic personality to have exercised over 'Abduh then and for many years afterwards so strange and so tenacious an influence. The link between them is very much that of the master and disciple in some secret, esoteric cult. One curious aspect of Afghani's appeal for the young 'Abduh was that he made himself out to be sexually impotent; Afghani, according to 'Abduh, "had lost the need and the capacity for marriage owing to his preoccupation with great things".[25] This reputation for sexual impotence Afghani was at some pains to foster; while in Istanbul, he vehemently refused the gift of a woman from Sultan

Abdul Hamid's harem, saying that he did not have the capacity for sexual intercourse, and threatening that if the Sultan insisted on pressing the gift upon him, Afghani would "cut the organ of procreation" and become a eunuch.[26] Again, Shakib Arslan, who as a young man knew Afghani in his last years at Istanbul, is emphatic that the only pleasures which counted with him were exclusively those of the intellect. He reports that when a Damascene asked Afghani, in his own presence, why he was not marrying and leaving a progeny, Afghani was quite disgusted, and after his departure remarked: "The spirit of philosophy has not penetrated into this nation". Shakib Arslan also reports the episode of Abdul Hamid's attempted gift of a woman and reports Afghani refusing the Sultan's bounty in these terms: "I have spent all my life like a bird on a branch, and I do not want at the end of my days to be tied down to a family."[27] It is a measure of Afghani's esoteric duplicity that such a remark can be interpreted in two opposite ways: that while Afghani was anxious to impress his ascetic self-denial on a respectful audience, he may also secretly have meant by it that he had enjoyed casual *liaisons* too much to be bothered at his time of life with maintaining an elaborate gynaeceum. For he was not sexually impotent: the terms of a letter written to him in July, 1885 (?) by a European woman called Kathi are such as to leave no doubt that in sexual matters Afghani was in fact rather a Tartuffe and something of a lady-killer.*

Whatever arts and stratagems Afghani employed to acquire and keep a following, there is no doubt that his disciples were bound to him by strong and peculiar ties of love and adoration. 'Abduh's feeling for him, in particular, was akin to idolatry. One of his students many years later recounted that when 'Abduh mentioned Afghani, which he did but seldom and that briefly, he would be seized with a "strong trembling" and tears would come to his eyes; this student further recalled that 'Abduh told them that his relation to Afghani was not merely that of a disciple to his master, or of a brother to his brother, "but was a relation of love which had overwhelmed the heart".[28] The tone which 'Abduh employed

* Iraj Afshar and Asghar Mahdavi, *Documents inédits concernant Seyyed Jamal al-Din Afghani*, Tehran 1963, hereafter referred to as *Documents*, plates 141–144: "Mon cher Din qui était pour Kathi tout ensemble qui t'aimais (*sic*) comme plus personne dans le monde peut t'aimer . . . j'espère que bientôt je peux te revoir mon adorable Gemal Ed din, mon Dieu mon Tout dans le monde . . . mille baisers de ta Kathi qui est à toi de corps et l'âme (*sic*)".

towards Afghani is strange enough. In 1874, 'Abduh wrote his first work, a short essay entitled *Risalat al-waridat,* or *Treatise of Mystical Inspirations.* In his preface he says that he had long been roaming in the fields of knowledge and had come upon the trace of "the true science"; he was taken with a great love for it, but was told that it was a sin to devote himself to it and that those who taught the dogmas of religion forbade its study. He became despondent at this prohibition and at "the limited mentality" shown by the teachers who discouraged originality and remained content with mechanical repetition. He continues,

"While I found myself in this state, the arrival of the perfect Sage, of Truth personified, of our venerated master Sayyid Jamal al-Din al-Afghani who does not cease to garner the fruits of science, made the sun of truths rise for us which illuminated the most complicated problems."[29]

This is not oriental hyperbole: "perfect Sage", "Truth personified", "the true science" have the unmistakable esoteric and heterodox ring. There is more to confirm such a view. In 1883, 'Abduh addressed a letter from Beirut, where he was living out his term of exile, to Afghani in Paris. Rashid Rida, who prints it in the second volume of his *Tarikh* is puzzled and scandalised by it. He calls it the strangest thing which 'Abduh ever wrote and likens the terms which 'Abduh uses to describe Afghani to the language of those sufi mystics who believed that God's was the only real existence; such language, even used in the way of poetic hyperbole, says Rashid Rida, is most unexpected in 'Abduh. He had good reason for his amazement, for 'Abduh says to Afghani:

"You have made us with your hands, invested our matter with its perfect form, and created us in the best shape . . . Through you have we known the whole universe";

and again,

'I have been endowed by you with a wisdom which enables me to change inclinations, impart rationality to reason, overcome great obstacles, and control the innermost thoughts of men.",

and again,

"I have been given by you a will so powerful as to move the immovable, deal blows to the greatest of obstacles, and remain firm in the right (*haqq*) until truth (*haqq*) is satisfied", etc. etc.*

---

* See Appendix I for a translation of the whole relevant passages.

This is the language of worship, but with this *'alim*, this man of religion, it is the language of idolatry.

Why should Afghani be so idolised, and what cult was 'Abduh celebrating? The doctrine which 'Abduh sought to prove, under Afghani's influence, in *Risalat al-waridat* seems to have been the heterodox doctrine of *Wahdat al-wujud;* it is summarised for us by B. Michel and Moustapha Abdel Razik: it is to the effect "that there is but one real existence, that of God"—the very doctrine, we may observe, the traces of which Rashid Rida saw to his scandal in 'Abduh's letter to Afghani.[30] The authors go on to say that

> "This is a widespread doctrine among the mystics, but which is rejected by the orthodox as tainted with heresy, because it tends to obliterate the difference between Creator and creation so emphatically asserted by Islam, and ends by leading to pantheism."[31]†

The exotic visitant in Cairo was evidently leading the young and fervent Azhar scholar to the dizzy heights of some spinozism. No wonder 'Abduh found the mentality of his teachers rather limited. But it is clear that the master was not content that the disciple should rest in some kind of crypto-pantheism; he must be led on, and allowed to see reality naked and without a veil. The next step in 'Abduh's philosophical progress is marked by a commentary which he wrote in 1876 on a well-known theological work, *al-'Aqa'id al-'adudiyya* by Jamal al-Din al-Iji. In this commentary, 'Abduh adopted a sceptical and properly "philosophical" view of religion. Commenting on the saying of the Prophet Muhammad that his community would in due course divide into seventy-three sects, and that only one of them was destined to salvation, 'Abduh took the line that there was nothing in the Prophet's

---

† *Wahdat al-wujud* was the heresy of pantheistic monism for which the Mughal Emperor Aurangzib condemned and executed Akbar's grandson Dara Shikoh (1615–1659) who was much influenced by Hindu philosophy and mysticism. Some lines from a poem by him may sum up this doctrine:
> O you, in quest of God, you seek Him everywhere,
> You verily are the God, not apart from Him!
> Already in the midst of the boundless ocean,
> Your quest resembles the search of a drop for the ocean!

Afghani, it is interesting to remember, spent some time in India in the 1850's and 'Anhuri, a member of his Cairo circle, specifically notes the Indian origin of some of his teachings. See Rashid Rida's *Tarikh*, vol. I, pp. 42–3. On the doctrine see further article "Allah" in *Enyclopaedia of Islam*, 2nd. ed.

saying to help us decide which of the sects will attain salvation. This, if creditably broad-minded, went clean against the orthodoxy in which 'Abduh had been brought up and which his diploma as *'alim* declared him fit to expound, since the orthodox doctors claimed to define salutary truth and damnable error and allowed no doubt in the matter. Again in the commentary, 'Abduh argued that any statement in the Qur'an had to conform to the canons of reason and that, if the literal sense of any statement did not conform, then an interpretation of the Qur'an's text must be sought which would reconcile it with the demands of reason!³² In thus progressing from pantheist mysticism to scepticism, 'Abduh exemplifies a common development in the history of religious belief. It is not surprising that neither *Risalat al-waridat* nor this commentary were published when they were written: indeed the first appeared posthumously and the second in the year of the author's death. But 'Abduh's heterodoxy could not have been a secret to his associates. In a lecture at the Egyptian University in 1922 Shaikh Mustafa Abd al-Raziq describes the doubtful reputation which the young *'alim* had in the traditional circles of al-Azhar in the 1870s, the result of his political articles in the newspaper *al-Ahram*,

"his association with Afghani, his interest in *falsafa*, his advocacy of certain mu'tazilite principles, his prohibition of traditional interpretation (*taqlid*), his call for the study of modern sciences, his preference for the sciences of the Franks, and also letting his hair grow long [presumably like a dervish]".³³

Another testimony comes from a European source, and is all the more significant because its author can have had little appreciation of the theological and doctrinal issues between Afghani and 'Abduh on the one hand, and their traditionalist adversaries on the other.

"His unselfish patriotism," wrote Broadley, 'Urabi's and 'Abduh's lawyer in 1882, "alone prevented some of his more fervent associates from openly resenting his more than suspected unorthodoxy. Even his friend Arabi had said once upon a time that 'Sheikh Abdu's head was better fitted for a hat than a turban'."³⁴

There is further evidence of 'Abduh's heterodoxy, relating to his years of exile. In 1884, while on a visit to London, 'Abduh, as Blunt records, had a discussion with Mirza Baqir on the nature of the Qur'an. Mirza Baqir, Professor Browne's Persian teacher, was a religious eclectic who was "successively a Shi'ite, a Muhammadan, a dervish, a Christian, an atheist, and a Jew", and had finished "by elaborating a religious system of his own which he called 'Islamo-Christianity'."[35] He seems to have been a familiar of Afghani's circle in Paris,[36] and he conformed, in his latitudinarianism, to a certain type of person who, as will be seen, continuously crops up in Afghani's *entourage*. 'Abduh and Mirza Baqir discussed on that occasion whether the Qur'an was originally a book, or only a compilation of oral sentences. "Abdu," writes Blunt, "holds the latter opinion, and I am quite with him, but the old Mirza is stiff as to its being a miraculous book."[37] To judge by Blunt's report, 'Abduh's discussion with Mirza Baqir turned on the ancient controversy between orthodox and mu'tazilites, whether the Qur'an was uncreated or created; and 'Abduh, if Blunt is to be believed, is here adopting a mu'tazilite position. Blunt's report is authoritatively confirmed by 'Abduh himself. After parting from Afghani in 1885, 'Abduh went to Beirut where he was asked to teach in *al-madrasa al-sultaniyya*. He there delivered some lectures on philosophical theology which were published twelve years afterwards, in 1897, as *Risalat al-tauhid*. A feature of the *Risala* is that it insists, in a manner reminiscent of Afghani, on the social utility of religion. The prophetic office, argues 'Abduh, enables society to maintain itself and to avoid calamity and anarchy; religion, in fact, is a good substitute for the natural feelings of love and sympathy between individuals which ordinarily do constitute and maintain the bonds of society.[38] In this *Risala*, 'Abduh maintains the position he took up in his controversy with Mirza Baqir; to believe the doctrine that the Qur'an was uncreated and had subsisted from all eternity was "to profess an error greater than all the erroneous doctrines which the Qur'an had refuted"; 'Abduh does admit that certain *imams* have refused to accept that the Qur'an was created: the reason for this, he claims,

> "was their desire to abstain in so passionate a quarrel and their excessive politeness towards their adversaries; we cannot", he continues, "explain this otherwise, for we think that the *imam* Ibn Hanbal was too distinguished a mind to believe that the Qur'an is uncreated . . ."[39]

When we remember that Ibn Hanbal went to prison and submitted to torture rather than concede that the Qur'an was created, we can but marvel at so bland and disingenuous a misrepresentation of his position, and at the fact that two years after the publication of such a passage, its author should have been appointed Mufti of Egypt. No wonder that, as Rashid Rida complained, the *Risala* was denounced by 'Abduh's adversaries as *mu'tazilite* in tendency.[40] Such accusations must have affected 'Abduh for, though he did not in so many words retract his doctrine, he admitted that the passage was controversial and ordered that it should not appear in subsequent editions; his disciple Rashid Rida took care to excise it,[41] and the passage now appears only in the French translation which was presumably made from the first edition.

It is clear that by the end of the 1870s the erstwhile mystic, outwardly a divine, was secretly a free thinker, like his master. For there is little doubt that Afghani was also secretly a freethinker and a sceptic where Islam as a dogma and a positive religion was concerned. His is not an isolated case. Readers of Professor Browne's *Year among the Persians* will remember how many concealed freethinkers, sceptical *sufis* and antinomian dervishes Browne met in his travels in the year 1889; and Mrs. Keddie, in her paper cited above,[42] has pointed to many examples of Persian divines who had lost their faith, and who yet remained outwardly pious, and even used their reputation and standing as men of religion to rouse the people against the autocracy of the Shah. Dealing with Afghani in particular, Miss Haim quotes many of his sayings the burden and import of which are unmistakable. One in particular may be cited here once again to give the keynote of his doctrine.

"There are two kinds of philosophy in the world", a Persian friend reported him saying, "one of them is to the effect that there is nothing in the world which is ours, so we must remain content with a rag and a mouthful of food. The other is to the effect that everything in the world is beautiful and desirable, that it does and ought to belong to us. It is the second which should be our ideal, to be adopted as our motto. As for the first, it is worthless, and we must pay no attention to it."[43] Further evidence can be quoted. A saying is attributed to him which dates from his Cairo period when his influence over 'Abduh was so great. It describes with remarkable precision 'Abduh's spiritual progress as it is exhibited in his early treatises. Afghani used to say:

"If a philosopher puts on rough clothing, lengthens his rosary and spends his time in the mosque then he is a mystic (*sufi*); but if he sits in Matatia's coffee-house [which Afghani

used to frequent with his circle] and smokes the hubble-bubble, then he remains only a philosopher".[44]
'Abd al-Qadir al-Maghribi recounts two stories which Afghani used to tell which illustrate his contempt for the credulous mass of believers and his sceptical relativism. The first story was of an incident which befell Afghani while on a ship which found itself in difficulties. His fellow-passengers were in a panic and Afghani reassured them by affirming that the ship would not sink. He was believed because, wearing a green turban, he was taken for a fakir able to foretell the future:

> "The matter was as simple as an exercise in arithmetic", Afghani went on, "for if the ship were to sink nobody would survive to give me the lie, whilst if it did not I would have attained sanctity by an easy process"!

The second story which Afghani used to tell concerned a believer and an unbeliever. The believer would exhort the unbeliever to pray by telling him:

> "Try to pray regularly for forty days, and see whether you can give up prayer afterwards"; to which the unbeliever retorted: "Give up praying for forty days, and see whether you can ever resume the practice afterwards"![45]

The Syrian Muhammad al-Makhzumi who knew him in his last days at Istanbul reports Afghani as saying that all three religions, Islam, Judaism and Christianity, were in perfect agreement in their principle and their purpose: they are complementary rather than in opposition. When he was young, Afghani said, he had looked forward to the union of the three religions, but found this afterwards to be impracticable owing to the dissensions promoted by the men of religion. 'Abduh, it is significant to remember, also at one time during his exile in Beirut, held such a belief and tried to promote this kind of religious union.[46] This emphasis on similarity between the three religions, we must be careful to note, is not so much an argument in favour of practical toleration, as a doctrinal rejection more or less extreme, of the positive dogmas which, for their followers, were, in effect, Judaism, Christianity and Islam. The rejection appears at its most extreme in Afghani's comment on Renan's lecture *L'Islamisme et la science*, where he accuses all revealed religions of obscurantism; it is more circumspectly phrased when 'Abduh, in a controversy with the Christian writer Farah Antun, claims that religion and science are entirely congruent with one another, and that the elements in religion which do not accord with philosophy are the fruit of superstition.[47] In fact, the emphasis on doctrinal similarity is a disguised plea for a new rationalist religion. What is even more interesting than the religion itself, is the sustained and ultimately successful attempt by Afghani and his disciples to deny all accusations of heterodoxy and to pass off their belief as orthodoxy itself.

The precise nature of a Muslim's religious belief today usually neither hinders nor advances his political prospects, but it was otherwise in Afghani's and 'Abduh's days, hence the great importance which both attached to a reputation of orthodoxy; and hence, consequently, the necessity for us to compare their outward professions and their inner thoughts, and to set side by side with their later reputation the testimony of those who knew and associated with them. Afghani's reputation for unbelief and heterodoxy pursued him all his life; the witnesses are too numerous and too unanimous for this to be a mere calumny and fabrication. He left Constantinople for Cairo in 1871 because he was attacked for heresy. In Egypt, the writer 'Abbas Mahmud al-'Aqqad tells us, Afghani had a reputation for heresy (*zandaqa*) among the divines. 'Aqqad allows us a glimpse of the kind of teaching which gave Afghani this reputation. Someone who used to be a member of Afghani's circle in Cairo recounted that one day the Master, discoursing on the subject of vices, declared that they were of two kinds, one which harmed both the body and the "rational soul", and another which harmed only the body, but left the "rational soul" intact, whereupon Ibrahim al-Halbawi, then one of his disciples, pertly said: "Fancy! and are the Sayyid's vices of the second kind?"[48]

In Cairo "he mixed with the dogma", writes his contemporary Abdullah al-Nadim, who was not an enemy,

"what gave rise to criticism . . . and some of his disciples became known for their heresy and for their great opposition to religion, either through misunderstanding or perverse teaching, so that many of the believers turned away from him."[49]

His friend and *protégé*, Adib Ishaq wrote that Afghani

"delved deeply into the traditional and rational sciences. The views of the ancient philosophers took hold of him and he became somewhat tinged with something of sufism."[50]

"He became expert in the study of religion", wrote Salim al-'Anhuri "until this led him to atheism and belief in the eternity of the world. He claimed that vital atoms, found in the atmosphere, formed, by a natural evolution the stars, which we see and which revolve round one another through magnetism, and that the belief in an all-knowing First Cause was a natural delusion which arose when man was in a primitive state of evolution and corresponded with the stage which his intellectual progress had reached."

It is significant and highly interesting that when 'Abduh came to Beirut on his exile, he induced 'Anhuri to publish a declaration saying that what he had related concerning Afghani's belief he had only heard from some Egyptians and Syrians, but that now 'Abduh had explained the true position. The libel, it now seemed, had originated with some followers whom Afghani had accepted in the goodness of his heart and who, when misfortunes befell him and he was expelled from Egypt, "started boasting of being his disciples, and ascribing to him their heretical opinions"![51] In the biographical notice which 'Abduh himself wrote he was quite circumspect in his treatment of this topic. People, he says, were jealous of him, and spread calumnies about him, taking for pretext his study of philosophical works which some late divines had forbidden reading.

"But those who would prohibit did not make the prohibition absolute; they limited it to those whose intellect is feeble and understanding limited; this was because they were afraid that the faith of such people might be perverted. As for those who are firm in their faith, they are permitted to study the sciences of the ancients and the moderns, whether these sciences agree or do not agree with their faith. This will but make them more knowledgeable about their faith, and firmer in their belief."[52]

The argument, it will be noticed, is studiously oblique; couched in generalities, it is careful to eschew the specific, and to avoid outright categorical denial. Seen in the light of 'Abduh's early treatises, the passage is ambiguous and equivocal. After being expelled from Egypt, Afghani went to Hyderabad, and an Indian Muslim, who knew him there, reported that "I gathered from his information that he was a free-thinker of the French type".[53] Again, in his last days in Istanbul, Afghani seems to have been party to the publication of a highly obscene attack on Abu'l Huda al-Sayyadi written by his protégé, al-Nadim, which was entitled *al-Masamir, The Nails;* the authors of a pamphlet written in reply, accuse him, among other things, of "having donned the mantle of philosophy."[54]

The company which Afghani kept also makes the orthodoxy of this professed divine highly suspect. From 1871, when he came to Egypt, until 1878, when he began his open political activity, Afghani was the centre of a group of intellectual malcontents and religious rebels, to whom he purveyed secret and subversive philosophical doctrines. In a society where tradition, though beginning to be seriously challenged, was still outwardly impregnable, his company and his teaching must have been like forbidden fruit, exhilarating and enormously attractive. One writer describes how Afghani used to keep to his house during the daytime, and only sally out at night, to hold long sessions with his disciples in a coffee-shop, smoking and drinking tea incessantly, occasionally indulging in a glass of brandy, and going back home only at dawn.[55] Another writer affords us a tantalising glimpse of Afghani and his band of rebellious Azharites visiting a bar in the Azbakiyya gardens in Cairo which had a beautiful European barmaid with whom Afghani, his reputation for impotence notwithstanding, to the delight of his disciples jocularly flirted.[56] Of these disciples, 'Abduh was only one, albeit subsequently the best-known; there was also 'Abdullah al-Nadim who had been destined by his father to the career of *'alim*, and who, disliking the prospect, ran away from home, spent many years as an itinerant versifier entertaining village notables at their drinking parties, and who later became a newspaper editor and the ablest and most prolific of 'Urabi's propagandists.[57] There was, again, the Syrian Christian writer Adib Ishaq (1856-1885), who seems to have been a radical in religion as well as in politics. He frequently attacked intemperately the Catholic and Maronite clergy.[58] When he died in Beirut, the clergy refused to pray for him, or to allow his body into a church unless his father signed a declaration that his son lived and died a Catholic; this was apparently not forthcoming for, according to the Jesuit Cheikho, Adib Ishaq was given a civil burial.[59] Again, we may mention the Jewish James Sanua (1839-1912), who claimed to have taught Afghani French while he was in Cairo. Sanua started his career as an ambulent actor, performing before popular audiences; like Nadim he became a newspaperman and, following obscure and perhaps shady transactions in which he was involved with the Khedive, he started, under Afghani's and 'Abduh's inspiration, to write against Isma'il who expelled him from Egypt in 1878. Sanua also was a promoter of religious union as understood by Afghani. No doubt to justify his religious views he used to tell how his mother, made desperate by losing several children in infancy, went to consult a Muslim holy man who told her that her next child would survive, but should be brought up to know Islam and the Qur'an. For this reason, Sanua used to say, he was brought up equally at home in Judaism, Christianity and Islam. It is an unlikely story, but the fact remains that the first leading article in *Abu Naddara*, the journal Sanua started in opposition to Isma'il, took the line that religious differences no longer mattered to the Egyptians, to the extent that they considered "Man" an adequate description for all men, and that all were brothers in humanity; again, one of the grievances which Sanua said he had against Isma'il was that the Khedive was inflaming the fanaticism of the Egyptians which Sanua and his friends had done their best to quench.[60] We come upon this "religion of humanity" in another of Afghani's associates, Malkam Khan, Armenian by origin, convert to Shi'ism, Persian Ambassador in London, who fell out with the Shah in 1889—a lottery concession granted to him having been annulled—and started publishing newspapers against Nasir al-Din in which Afghani was, for some time, associated.

"Malkam", writes Professor Keddie, "was nominally a Moslem of Christian descent, but he worked to spread a 'religion of humanity', which he thought would present Western ideas to Iranians in religious terms that would make them more acceptable, and most reliable informants believe he was a freethinker".[61]

We may mention as another of Afghani's heterodox associates the Reverend Louis Sabunji, a Catholic priest from North Mesopotamia, who served for a time in the Propaganda at Rome and who seems to have been involved in a religious altercation at Beirut in the mid-eighteen seventies, in the course of which he was attacked by the mob and had to leave the city.[62] According to Wilfrid Blunt, who employed him as oriental secretary, he had "thrown off the cassock" and was "much more in sympathy with Islam than with his own faith". Blunt writes that Sabunji's newspaper *al-Nahlah, The Bee*, which appeared in London preached "religious reform on the most advanced lines of modern thought"; the numbers of *al-Nahlah* extant show nothing of the kind, except perhaps an article in the number of 1 February 1879 which attacked religious differences under the title *al-Taqsim asl al-fasad, Discord is the source of decay*, and it is probable that Blunt reported Sabunji's views not as they appeared in *al-Nahlah*—he could not read Arabic—but as they were communicated to him orally.[63]

c

But *al-Nahlah* shows that Sabunji was very quick to protest against Afghani's expulsion, for in October 1879 *al-Nahlah* published a eulogy of *al-failasuf*, the thinker Jamal al-Din, deploring the action of the Egyptian Government against one who was labouring for progress, unity and freedom. Finally, Afghani's associates during his last years in Istanbul included, as Professor Keddie in her article shows, Persian Babis prominent in the dissemination of heterodoxy, and active in subverting the authority of the Persian Government.

When Afghani was expelled from Egypt, the British Consul-General, reporting the event and giving details of Afghani's history as they were no doubt current in official circles, wrote that he "was recently expelled from the Freemasons' Lodge at Cairo, of which he was a member, on account of his open disbelief in a Supreme Being."[64] For Afghani was indeed a freemason and the fact is highly significant. Freemasonry and freethinking seem to have been closely linked at that time in the Near East. To be a freemason was to show one's dislike of orthodox, traditional religion, the power it gave to ecclesiastics, and the hatreds and divisions it promoted and perpetuated in society. Malkam Khan was a freemason, Adib Ishaq was one, James Sanua likewise.[65] The reputation of masons for heterodoxy has been recorded by Jurji Zaydan, himself most probably a mason:

"As for the vulgar mass", he wrote, "it is useless to ask how deeply ingrained in their minds was hatred and contempt for the sect of the masons; it was so to such an extent that the term became a synonym for the expression of hatred and contempt. If they wished to describe how heinously atheistical or hypocritical somebody was, they found no better term to describe him than the word, freemason".[66]

Freemasonry seems to have been introduced into the Near East by the French. Masonic tradition has it that Bonaparte founded a lodge in Cairo according to the Rite of Memphis in 1798; whether this is so or not, it is possible that the Saint-Simonians, who took refuge in Egypt from their vicissitudes in France, either continued the tradition or effectively started it.[67] French freemasonry was divided into two bodies, the larger of which was the Grand Orient dating from the eighteenth century, and the General Scotch Lodge dating from 1804. Lodges in Egypt—and in Syria—seem to have been affiliated some to the Grand Orient and some to the General Scotch Lodge. In 1877, the Grand Orient, after many years' discussion, decided that masons should no longer be required to believe in the existence of the Grand Architect of the Universe, as a condition of membership. This decision precipitated a rupture of relations between the United Grand Lodge of England and the Grand Orient to the benefit of the General Scotch Lodge, which continued to require belief in the Grand Architect as a condition of membership.[68] Is it the echo of this dispute which, reverberating in the Egyptian lodges, finally reaches us in Lascelles' despatch as the report of Afghani's expulsion from "the Freemasons Lodge at Cairo, of which he was a member, on account of his open disbelief in a Supreme Being"? It is most likely, for the Arabic sources tell us that Afghani was a member of the Scotch Lodge, had a disagreement with his fellow-members, seceded from it, and established a Lodge which he affiliated to the Grand Orient, of which he became the master, and which had branches in ministries and government offices.[69] When Afghani was expelled from Egypt, the police also confiscated documents belonging to 'Abduh; among the papers which they took away, as 'Abduh later informed Afghani, was "the book of the masons by the hand of my exalted lord".[70] Did this book contain the regulations of Afghani's lodge?

Whether Afghani did not believe in the existence of the Grand Architect, or whether he thought that belief in him was not necessary in a mason, we cannot say. In later years, he was anxious to emphasise that masons required their adherents to believe in the existence of God and the immortality of the soul.[71] Considering the man's fondness for oblique discourse, and bearing in mind the allegation contained in Lascelles' despatch, we may perhaps be justified in suspecting the inaccuracy of Afghani's statement to be deliberate, and significant as an attempt indirectly to refute a scandalous accusation. In any case, his secession from the Lodge and his affiliation to the Grand Orient is indication enough of his radicalism. It cannot be doubted that he saw in masonry a modern extension of ancient Islamic heterodoxy to which he was clearly attracted. In an application to join a masonic Lodge in Egypt in 1875,[72] he describes himself as a "teacher of philosophical sciences" and addresses the Masons as *"ikhwan al-safa . . . wa khullan al-wafa"* i.e. "sincere brethren . . . and faithful companions", clearly in deliberate allusion to the famous Isma'ili treatise.

When he was expelled from Egypt, the Cairo French newspaper *La Réforme* commented that Afghani's "liberal and indifferentist rather than irreligious tendencies"[73] were not the main cause of his expulsion; the same may perhaps be said of his masonic adventures: belief or non-belief in a Grand Architect may not wholly explain them. In a letter written at Port Said on his way to Europe at the end of 1882, Afghani complains—and the complaint must seem significant—that when he was expelled from Egypt in 1879 he was unjustly accused of being the master of a Masonic lodge which had for its basis "the ruin of religion and the world (*fasad al-din wa'l-dunia*)".[74] Both 'Abduh, from his own knowledge, and Makhzumi, on Afghani's authority, affirm that his purpose in the masonic lodge was political.[75] Makhzumi says that Afghani left his original lodge because he objected to a brother saying that masonry was not concerned with politics. Rashid Rida, again, in an obituary notice published on 'Abduh's death, the details of which, it is interesting to observe, he omitted from the biography, wrote that Afghani initiated 'Abduh into masonry:

"I asked him ['Abduh] once what masonry really was, and he said that its rôle—now ended—in the countries in which it is found was to resist the authority of kings and popes who were fighting against knowledge and freedom, and that this was a great achievement and one of the pillars of European progress . . . He also told me that his membership and the Sayyid's [Afghani] was for a political and social purpose."[76]

The secret subversive work of Oriental masons was indeed known to Oriental rulers and troubled them. As early as 1861 we find Shah Nasir al-Din issuing dire warnings against membership in the *faramushkaneh*.[77] The head of the Persian freemasons at that time was Malkam Khan's father, and Malkam Khan himself told Blunt that his "religion of humanity" was meant to prepare the Persians for political action by way of religious reform.[78] Freemasonry was in equally bad odour with the Ottoman authorities immediately before the Young Turk Revolution and earlier.[79] In Egypt itself, a decade or so before Afghani's activities, there was suspicion that Prince Halim, Muhammad Ali's youngest son, who was Grand Master of the Order, was using masonry to forward his ambitions to the Khediviate. In 1868, Isma'il exiled him and the lodges were closed. It was not until four years later that the Khedive sanctioned their revival.[80]

Afghani, then, was not a Jean Meslier secretly elaborating in a country presbytery an infidel doctrine and desiring with quiet desperation that the last king should be strangled with the intestines of the last priest.[81] His history shows him to have been a confirmed doer, fertile in expedients and stratagems, equally adept at the traditional methods of oriental statecraft and at the newer techniques made possible by the spread of literacy and of printing. From 1871, when he settled in Egypt, until 1878, as has been seen, little is heard of him. But 'Anhuri allows us a glimpse into his activities. Through his connexions with Riad he obtained permission for Adib Ishaq to publish in Cairo a newspaper, *Misr* which propagated his views and in which he himself wrote pseudonymous articles. He then directed Adib Ishaq to publish another newspaper in Alexandria, *al-Tijara*, in which his followers 'Abduh and Laqqani were ordered to collaborate. They created, says 'Anhuri, a reputation for him in Egypt by means of the extravagant eulogies with which they lauded him in these newspapers; they called him, for instance, the "repository of wisdom's secrets" and the "astrolabe [disclosing the movement of] the heavenly bodies of the sciences." It was in 1878, 'Anhuri continues, that Afghani assumed public importance because he took part in politics and became the president of the "Arab masonic society."[82] The year 1878 saw Egypt enter on a period of political turbulence which gave Afghani his opportunity. Internally, Isma'il's financial maladministration was slowly but inexorably involving him and his subjects in a fearful crisis; externally, the hostilities between Russia and the Porte which began in 1876, Midhat Pasha's *coup d'état*, the proclamation of the Ottoman Constitution, the Congress of Berlin and all the attendant excitements could not but unsettle a Muslim country accustomed to give allegiance to the Sultan and to sustain his cause against the Christian Powers. In April 1878 Isma'il was compelled by the agitation of his creditors and the pressure of the Powers to agree to the appointment of a Commission to enquire into the financial position of Egypt. Riad Pasha and Sir Rivers Wilson were appointed Vice-Presidents of this Commission. The enquiry was highly unwelcome to Isma'il since it exposed his extortions and malversations. If Riad, the only Egyptian member of the Commission, were to take his duties in earnest, he would be likely to draw upon himself the anger and displeasure of the Khedive. In the event, for whatever reason, Riad played his part equally with all other members in the work of the Commission.

> "At a time when any show of independent opinion on the part of an Egyptian was accompanied with a good deal of personal risk", wrote Cromer, a fellow-member of the Commission, "Riaz Pasha displayed a high degree of moral courage. His

presence on the Commission was of material help to his colleagues, whose confidence he fully deserved and obtained."[83]

The Commission reported in August. One of their main conclusions was that the estates of the Khedive and his family should be ceded to the State, and that he should accept the principle of ministerial responsibility. Isma'il had no alternative but to agree, and on August 28 he invited Nubar Pasha to form a ministry, the collective advice of which he engaged himself to accept. In this ministry Riad became Minister of the Interior.

It soon became clear that Isma'il would not readily acquiesce in sudden and total deprivation both of power and of wealth. He began complaining of his Ministers, of their want of confidence in him and of their desire to reduce him to a cipher. The British Consul-General reported in January 1879 that the Khedive was secretly encouraging opposition in the Chamber of Notables to the measures of the Nubar Ministry;[84] a few weeks later, on 18 February, Nubar and Sir Rivers Wilson, his Minister of Finance, were assaulted by a mob of officers protesting against arrears in pay. Isma'il thereupon declared that he would not be responsible for public order, unless Nubar resigned. Nubar did so, and Isma'il was for the moment triumphant. There is little doubt that the officers' mutiny was contrived or connived at by the Khedive, who thus unleashed the forces which later, under 'Urabi's leadership, came near to abolishing the Khediviate in Egypt.[85]

When Nubar's ministry was being reconstituted, the Khedive strenuously insisted that Riad should vacate the Interior and take over the Ministry of Foreign Affairs and Justice, but he was as strenuously resisted, and Riad for the time being remained to stand in Isma'il's way and prevent his total control of the provinces. With Nubar gone, Riad became the chief object of Isma'il's animosity. In a despatch of 1 April, 1879, the British Consul-General reported that meetings of notables and *'ulama* were being held at the house of Shaikh al-Bakri, *naqib al-ashraf*, the purpose of which was to stir up religious feelings against Wilson and de Blignières, the European Ministers whom Isma'il had agreed to appoint the previous August, and that Riad was being denounced in the mosques as a friend of the Christians; four days later, the Consul-General reported that there was no doubt that the Khedive was behind the agitation against Riad; and six days later, on 10 April, the Consul-General reported that Isma'il had ordered Riad to resign as vice-president of the Commission of enquiry, and that Riad had appealed to Sir Rivers Wilson for protection for himself and his family; finally on 22 April Riad left for Naples to remain in exile until Isma'il was deposed and Taufiq succeeded him.[86]

Afghani, it will be recalled, came to Egypt in 1871 under the patronage of Riad, and it is interesting to observe that in 1878-9 he appears on the political scene as an enemy of the Khedive Isma'il and therefore, in those circumstances, a supporter of Riad. He is found haranguing a crowd in Alexandria in these terms:

"Oh! you poor fellah! You break the heart of the earth in order to draw sustenance from it and support your family. Why do you not break the heart of your oppressor? Why do you not break the heart of those who eat the fruit of your labour?"[87]

When we remember the charges of extortion and oppression made against Isma'il and at that particular moment underlined by the conclusions of the Commission of Inquiry, there can be little doubt as to the identity of the oppressor whom Afghani denounced. But Afghani's opposition to Isma'il can be further illustrated. Muhammad 'Abduh told Blunt in 1903 that Afghani proposed to assassinate Isma'il and that he himself strongly approved; the Mufti added:

"If we had known Arabi at that time, we might have arranged it with him, and it would have been the best thing that could have happened, as it would have prevented the intervention of Europe. It would not, however, have been possible" he added, "to establish a republic in the then state of political ignorance of the people."[88]*

Again, in his biographical notice, 'Abduh writes that Afghani met Tricou, the French Consul-General, to urge Isma'il's deposition on him. This must have been between May, 1879, when Tricou was appointed, and the end of June when Isma'il was deposed. The detail is interesting, because of the two Powers then most interested in Egyptian affairs, France, in contrast to Great Britain, had little desire to treat Isma'il leniently, believing him to be mainly intent on defrauding his creditors, and Tricou furthermore was personally hostile to the Khedive, to an extent such that his appointment to Cairo was considered to indicate the French Government's

---

* 'Abduh was involved with Afghani in an incitement to assassination: *al-'Urwa al-wuthqa* no. 15, 28 August, 1884, asked whether no Egyptian was contemptuous enough of death to deal with Nubar, "this Armenian Minister".

displeasure with Isma'il.[89] Whether he worked to support Riad, or whether he hoped to see his own schemes prevail, the trend of Afghani's activities is unmistakable.

An examination of the origins of the so-called National Party in whose name 'Urabi later claimed to speak further illuminates Afghani's role in Egyptian politics. As has been seen, the first popular intervention in the Egyptian crisis was in February, 1879, when a mob of officers attacked Nubar and Wilson. The probable author and the undoubted beneficiary of this demonstration was the Khedive, and considering Afghani's opposition to Isma'il, it is most unlikely that he or his followers had anything to do with it. Neither does he seem to have taken part in another ostensibly popular initiative inspired beyond any reasonable doubt by the Khedive himself. Having got rid of Nubar, Isma'il proceeded to rid himself of the plan of the Commission of Inquiry to which he had agreed in the previous August. In April, 1879, Isma'il suddenly made public a project of financial reforms which he claimed to have gained the united suffrages of the chief men of Egypt. He sent to the representatives of the powers addresses signed by the *ulama* headed by the Shaikh of al-Azhar, Shaikh al-'Abbasi, by ministers and higher officials headed by Sharif Pasha, by high-ranking officers including 'Urabi* and his principal coadjutors in the mutiny of 1881, by notables and merchants; and, to impress the Powers with the unanimity of the Egyptians, the address included the signatures—almost statutory on such occasions—of the Coptic Patriarch and the Chief Rabbi.[90]† The addresses purported to reject the Commission's plan, and to pray him to put into effect in Egypt the Ottoman Constitution of 1877. Bowing to the unanimous wishes of his subjects, Isma'il dismissed the rump of Nubar's ministry which had survived the February incident, and appointed Sharif Pasha, a prominent petitioner, as his chief minister. The *coup d'état*, as Cromer calls it, availed Isma'il nothing, for this audacious attempt to hoodwink his creditors determined the Powers to make an end of him, and Isma'il was deposed.

* 'Urabi seems to have been in the Khedive's good books since Isma'il presented him with a slave from his harem, who became his wife. See Charles Royle, *The Egyptian Campaigns 1882 to 1885*, London, 1900, p. 16.

† In a memorandum (*Documents*, plates 101–105) Isma'il's agent, Ibrahim al-Muwailihi, claimed that it was he who organised the popular agitation on Isma'il's behalf. He published, on the Khedive's orders, a pamphlet against Riad and was rewarded by a post in the Ministry of Finance when Sharif took office.

Ismail's instrument in his last bid to resume unfettered control of Egypt was, then, Muhammad Sharif Pasha (1826-1887), who had been in the Khedivial service since 1863, and who, together with Nubar and Riad, was under Isma'il one of the usual contenders for chief ministerial office. Those who knew him seem agreed that he was entirely Isma'il's creature. Moberley Bell, the correspondent of *The Times*, called him a dummy and described him as completely under Isma'il's thumb;[91]

> "Cherif Pasha, minister of foreign affairs," wrote Baron des Michels, French Consul-General some time before these events, "was given the task of delaying action over consular representations, of interposing himself between the Consuls and the Khedive, to shield His Highness and draw attacks away from him. Cherif was a handsome man, holding very high an exceedingly empty head, full of his own importance, but really a nonentity."[92]

Sharif now appeared as the people's tribune, their champion against foreign greed and interference. This new role, suddenly assumed, clearly disconcerted some observers and we find Vivian, the British Consul-General, describing in his despatches Sharif and other officials under the Khedive's control alternately as the Turkish party, and as the National movement; for by their antecedents, associations and immediate interests, Sharif and his fellows were undoubtedly the court or Turkish party, while by their professions and outward behaviour they strove hard to pose as the defenders of the national interest and the popular welfare. These people constituted then and subsequently the National Party; with them 'Urabi and the other officers remained long associated; to them Afghani and his disciples, supporters of Riad, Sharif's exiled rival, were opposed.

Isma'il was deposed in June, 1879 and his eldest son Taufiq was proclaimed his successor. Naturally enough, neither Isma'il nor the men who had served him so long could bring themselves to believe that this was an irrevocable step or that Taufiq had the strength and the ability to inspire, while his father was still living, respect and loyalty in his servants. Sharif, the beneficiary of Isma'il's *coup d'état* in April, was still Chief Minister at Taufiq's accession. Soon afterwards, thinking to take advantage of Taufiq's weakness and inexperience, whether to pave the way for Isma'il's return or to increase his own power, Sharif submitted a project for a constitution. But Taufiq firmly rejected it, dismissed Sharif and, recalling Riad from exile, appointed him Chief Minister.[93]

In the interval between Sharif's dismissal in mid-August and Riad's assumption of power a month later, Taufiq dealt quite as firmly with another potential, if much less important, troublemaker. On 30 August he had Afghani arrested and sent out of the country. The biographical notices concerning Afghani collected by Rashid Rida in his *Tarikh* concur in stating that during the last months of Isma'il's reign Taufiq was under Afghani's influence and a member of his masonic lodge, and that on Taufiq's accession Afghani had an interview with the new Khedive in which he endeavoured to convert Taufiq to his views. It does seem to be the case that Taufiq and his father were not on good terms, and it is likely that in the last agitated months of Isma'il's reign, Taufiq should have encouraged by present favour and promise of future performance, a group dedicated to the overthrow of his father. It is quite as likely that on his accession, Afghani should have thought it easy, with his masonic apparatus infiltrating the ministries, to become a power in the land. It is interesting that the correspondent of *The Times*, in reporting Afghani's banishment, linked his name with that of Sharif. As has been seen, Sharif and Riad were rivals, Afghani was Riad's client, and it is highly unlikely that Afghani would have worked for Sharif when Riad was a power in the land; but with Isma'il deposed, Sharif in power and his rival still in exile, it may have seemed to Afghani that here was an interesting situation to be exploited. In a letter which he wrote to Riad from Port Said at the end of 1882, Afghani complains bitterly of "the officer 'Uthman" who, he says, was responsible for his expulsion.[94] It is most likely that this was 'Uthman Rifqi, the Minister of War. In his letter to Riad, Afghani claims that the masons, followers of Prince Abd al-Halim, were trying to make their patron Khedive, and that out of affection for Taufiq, he, Afghani, broke with them and incurred their enmity. They then began to spread calumnies against him, alleging that he wanted to kill the Khedive and the Consuls. Afghani goes on to say that 'Uthman helped the masons in their campaign, but that Sharif rebuked and made him desist. However, when he was dismissed 'Uthman was able to revenge himself on Afghani by procuring his expulsion. It would appear, then, from this passage that Sharif was protecting Afghani during his last months in Egypt, and that it was not the mere coincidence of their opposition to Taufiq which made the correspondent of *The Times* link their names.

It will be seen that in this letter, Afghani does not allege, as he was shortly afterwards to do, that he was expelled at the wish of the British government. For this allegation there is no basis; the despatch from the Consul-General reporting Afghani's expulsion records this as a decision taken by the Khedive against a troublemaker of which he had merely informed the British representative.95 What kind of trouble was Afghani making?

When Afghani was in Moscow in 1887, the *Moscow Gazette* of 1/13 July published a notice giving details of his career. The notice seems to have been based on information which he supplied, and therefore to be full of those familiar inventions which, in a most successful attempt to cover up his traces, he himself diligently and studiously spread. To help its readers place Afghani, the *Gazette* stated that he was mentioned in M. E. Vauquelin's *Memoirs of the Egyptian Revolution*.96 This bare reference must have seemed sufficient to the *Gazette*, but whatever Vauquelin's fame at that period, he is now sunk into obscurity. Ernest Vauquelin was a French left-wing journalist who wrote not a book, as might be supposed from the *Gazette's* reference, but a series of articles for the socialist newspaper, *L'Intransigeant*, which was founded and edited by Henri Rochefort. The series, *Souvenirs de la Révolution d'Egypte*, appeared in the summer and autumn of 1882, and both the title and the contents of the articles seem to indicate that the author witnessed some of the events which culminated in 'Urabi's *coup d'état* and the bombardment of Alexandria. At this point of time, Vauquelin's articles give us no new information, but merely constitute one more specimen, not particularly distinguished, of the radical and liberal version of Egyptian events and the policies of the powers with which W. S. Blunt and his numerous followers have made us so familiar. The second article of the series, published on 3 August, does, however, throw some new light on the circumstances of Afghani's expulsion from Egypt:

"One evening in the Hasan mosque in Cairo, before an audience of four thousand people", writes Vauquelin, "he (Afghani) gave a powerful speech in which he denounced with a deep prophetic sense three years before the event the utlimate purpose of British policy on the banks of the Nile.

"He also showed at the same time the Khedive Taufiq as compelled to serve—consciously or not—British ambitions, and ended his speech by a war-cry against the foreigner and by a call for a revolution to save the independence of Egypt and establish its liberty."

Vauquelin's account indicates why Taufiq thought Afghani's presence in Egypt dangerous to his régime.

Further evidence confirms such a view. The collection of *Documents* recently published contains a letter which his Egyptian disciple Ibrahim al-Laqqani sent him from his exile in Beirut on 15 February 1883. Laqqani had published the newspaper *Mir'at al-Sharq* in Cairo in 1879 under Afghani's inspiration, had gone under a cloud when his master was exiled, had regained favour under Riad's administration, had taken part in 'Urabi's rebellion and like 'Abduh had been tried and sent into exile. In this letter, the tone of which is as idolatrous as 'Abduh's, Laqqani speaks of the "speech of the Master(*khutbat al-maula*)" and of the prodigious effect it had had on a group of Syrian Christians in Alexandria who persuaded some Muslims to combine with them into a society in order to publish a newspaper, and to submit to Riad a plan of reforms.[97] Laqqani makes another remark which may throw some light on the relation between Sharif and Afghani, for he tells his master that the group of Syrian Christians at Alexandria and their paper were widely taken to represent Sharif's views and were therefore attacked by those who wanted to flatter Riad Pasha (when in fact they were only propagating Afghani's ideas). There is little doubt that Laqqani is here referring to the society known as the Young Egypt Party, and he is saying that the foundation of this society is the result of a speech of Afghani's. Is it not very likely that this is the speech which Vauquelin describes? If it is not, then it must have been a very similar one, and we must therefore conclude that at Taufiq's accession Afghani was making subversive speeches in mosques and other public places and inciting disaffection towards the ruler. Taufiq may have been afraid of even more extensive ambitions. 'Anhuri states that Taufiq suspected Afghani of wishing to change the Egyptian régime into a republican one of which he would be the head.[98]

But it was not his public speeches which the authorities adduced as the reason of Afghani's expulsion. The official announcement, published in the press on 28 August 1879, was a long document signed by the Director of Publications. The notice stated that the Government had seized documents belonging to Afghani which showed that he had organised a secret society composed of "young thugs" (*shubban dhawi al-batsh*), the aim of which was "the ruin of religion and rule". The document went on to say that Afghani had been expelled both from his own country and from Istanbul for similar offences and that by order of the Department of the Interior, he was now deported via Suez to the Hijaz.[99] Afghani, as has been seen, protested vigorously to an unknown correspondent against the accusation that he was conspiring to ruin religion and rule. You know, Afghani tells his correspondent, what our assembly (*majlis*) was in fact, what its basis was, and how corruption (*fasad*) crept into it; how then did you allow the officer 'Uthman to lie and allege that I was the president of an association (*majma*') which sought to ruin religion and rule?[100] The language of this letter inclines one to suspect that Afghani is here addressing a member of the masonic lodge he had founded, and that it was this lodge which the Egyptian authorities described as a society composed of young thugs. That the Egyptian authorities were not entirely wrong seems to be admitted by Afghani when he speaks of corruption creeping into his organisation.

When Afghani was banished from Egypt, his disciples also received the attentions of the police. 'Abduh, notably, was exiled to his village. His exile lasted for a year, and it seems to have been an unhappy period in his life.

"I was soon tired of being in my village", he told Blunt, "and went to Alexandria where I was watched by the police, so I went secretly to Tantah and wandered about for a long while".[101]

He then took up quarters in the house of Rifa'a Bey[102] on the outskirts of Cairo, reading in his library by day and going to Cairo in disguise by night. In his letter to Afghani from Beirut 'Abduh stated that his enemies were successful in turning Riad against Afghani and his disciples for a while when "he proceeded to deal harshly and severely with us".[103] If Afghani had combined with Sharif when Riad was an exile in Naples, then the Chief Minister's displeasure with Afghani's followers seems natural. But Riad at length relented and 'Abduh was through his kindness not only rescued from this uncomfortable clandestinity but also appointed an Editor in the official Gazette.[104]

It was during this period, when Afghani was far away in Hyderabad and 'Abduh a vagabond dodging the police, that the so-called National Party firmly took root and began to flourish in Egypt. Riad was Chief Minister, and all Isma'il's supporters and sympathisers now out of favour. A cabal of ex-ministers and placemen headed, it seems, by Sharif, Shahin Pasha Ghanj and 'Umar Pasha Lutfi organised opposition to Riad. The group was known as the Helwan society. Jean Ninet, an opponent of the régime and later a supporter of 'Urabi, who had dealings with the group, explains that they were so known because as a result of their activities they had to retire to Helwan, where the police kept them under observation.[105] They distributed in November 20,000 copies of a manifesto—the French version of which Ninet drew up—against Riad, and persuaded Adib Ishaq, the journalist, a follower of Afghani and hence of Riad, to forsake his old connexion and devote himself to Sharif's cause. His desertion still rankled four years afterwards in 'Abduh's mind, and in his letter to Afghani of 1883 previously cited, he speaks of him as a "base scoundrel" and denounces his "mean and treasonable" proceedings.[106] Riad shut down Adib's paper, and he was sent by Sharif's party to Paris where they subsidised his newspaper, *Misr al-Qahira*, which Adib filled with abuse of Riad.* It was not until Riad fell and Sharif became Chief Minister, this time a beneficiary of 'Urabi's *coup d'état*, that Adib Ishaq came back to Egypt when he was made a Bey, and appointed Director of the Government Translation and Publicity Office, and Secretary of the Chamber of Delegates.[107]

It is not necessary to assume that Sharif and his group were acting entirely on Isma'il's behalf, but that Isma'il encouraged such proceedings cannot be doubted. According to Rashid Rida, Isma'il subsidised Adib Ishaq in Paris, and 'Abduh told Blunt that when Sharif became Chief Minister in 1881 he helped Ratib Pasha, his son-in-law, who was Isma'il's agent, to engineer the ex-Khedive's restoration.[108] But the Helwan society, including as it did notables and landowners, was moved not only by the ambition to overthrow Riad and take his place, but also by dislike of Riad's administration, since Riad had abolished the employment of forced labour. Again, Isma'il's use of popular agitations in February and April 1879 had created a precedent for the use of this new and seemingly potent weapon. When 'Urabi and his fellow-officers, nursing their military grievances, mutinied against Riad and the Khedive in 1881, a junction was

---

* In a memorandum (*Documents*, plates 101–105), Ibrahim al-Muwailihi states that Isma'il sent him from Naples to Paris to get Adib Ishaq to serve his designs.

effected between them and the National Party proper, the civilian group, that is, known as the Helwan society. "It was I who created the National Party", Sharif said to Blunt in January, 1882, "and they will find that they cannot get on without me".[109] In this he was wrong, for in the alliance between the military and the Helwan society, it was inevitable that the officers should speedily gain the upper hand, and furthermore, they could use the slogans of independence and popular government as effectively as Sharif and his friends. But in this, at least, he was right that it was he and his supporters, not Afghani, not 'Abduh, not Riad's supporters, who had launched the National Party.

When Riad fell in September 1881, 'Abduh had been for some time Chief Editor of the official Gazette and member of the Higher Council for Education. He owed these favours to Riad, and, it would seem, to Riad's earlier connexion with Afghani. In his letter of 1883, cited above, 'Abduh tells Afghani that evil men

> "had turned His Excellency Riad Pasha against you, and against your true disciples for a little while during which," continued 'Abduh, no doubt referring to his wanderings in the Egyptian provinces, "he proceeded to deal harshly and severely with us. But we soon reached him after they had detained me in my birthplace and prohibited me from entering any city for some four months, clarified the matter and revealed the hidden truth so as to render ineffective the lies of the mendacious and harmless their intrigues, and all that they were doing; and I attained in his eyes a position which was the envy of the divines, of the military officers and of the officials"[110]

'Abduh deplored the downfall of Riad, and never had anything but praise for him; one of his rare attempts at poetry is a eulogy of Riad which he composed in prison awaiting trial after 'Urabi's rebellion.[111] At the outset, 'Abduh was opposed to 'Urabi and his friends. In the first place Sharif was now in power, and Sharif was Isma'il's supporter and Riad's opponent; and in the second, 'Urabi and the officers were a new unknown group whose intentions were not clear; he also looked down on them as an uncouth, untutored lot far from appreciating his master's philosophical views: he was, he told Afghani in the letter of 1883, engaged in propagating Afghani's doctrine and had fair hopes of success when "we were overborne by highwaymen intent on cutting the road leading to welfare; these men donned the garb of prophets but followed the methods of tyrants; they spoke the words of learned men and were inwardly ignorant; they adopted our manner of calling for liberty, and were enabled by the power of the sword and the weakness of the government to convince the vulgar mass that they stood for right and truth and the protection of the laws. At the outset," he continued, "their enmity towards you and towards your disciples was very great, and in this they were joined by those evil men and scoundrels whom we have mentioned before."[112]

This passage seems a cursory and cryptic account of the way in which the Helwan society propagated the political slogans which Afghani himself had adopted, of how they affected a juncture with the officers—"the power of the sword"—and of how some of Afghani's erstwhile disciples like Adib Ishaq—"those evil men and scoundrels"—had found it profitable to join the new masters. 'Abduh goes on to say that he worked to enlighten them and was hopeful of their realising Afghani's aims, were it not that 'Urabi showed himself to be an incompetent, falling between two stools, practising neither virtue nor unscrupulous power. This again is a cryptic account of his activities during the 'Urabi period. When he was charged with complicity in the rebellion, his defence was obedience to superior orders.

"Before the curtain rose", wrote his lawyer Broadley, "he had become the editor of the Egyptian *Official Gazette*, and in this capacity had from first to last obeyed the orders of his lawful superiors as they succeeded one another on the stage."[113]

We may reasonably assume that this was a line adopted in self-defence, but this need not mean that it is devoid of all truth, for 'Abduh, as his career shows, was not a masterful character, was rather inclined to follow a strong leadership, and adapt himself to the prevailing wind. It was so when he acquiesced in Afghani's plans and again when he became a supporter of Cromer and a friend of the English occupation. When Sharif succeeded Riad in September, 1881, much as he deplored the change, 'Abduh could very well have adapted himself to the new régime; the more so that he must have soon found the military, who were now the real rulers, fertile ground for Afghani's ideas. We can at any rate say that the new régime did not deprive him of his appointments, but that, on the contrary, as Blunt's diary shows, he was soon playing a prominent rôle as spokesman and go-between, and professing "a political creed akin to pure republicanism".[114]

The specific crime with which 'Abduh was charged at his trial after the collapse of the rebellion indicates his position and importance. He was accused of administering unlawful oaths, and though he endeavoured to minimise the importance of his actions, they do show him to have been at the very centre of the rebellion and in the confidence of its leaders. He alleged that as a result of some junior officers threatening the public order, Barudi, then Chief Minister, called upon him as a man of religion with a knowledge of the appropriate formulae, to administer an oath to these officers to bind them to keep the peace and obey military regulations. The facts seem to be otherwise. Those to whom 'Abduh administered the oath were not junior officers creating a disturbance, but the principal ministers and superior officers who were siding with 'Urabi. The occasion of the oath was a demand by the powers for the exile of 'Urabi and his fellow-officers, and its purpose was to bind all the participants to stand together and resist foreign intervention.[115] Ya'qub Sami, Under Secretary of War in the rebel government, when asked at the trial about this oath, said that he could not remember it but that it was a long masonic one, in which those who would betray their comrades were pronounced to deserve death and to have their tongue cut. 'Abduh, in his interrogatory, subsequently gave a version of the oath, and this version stipulated that the penalty for breaking it was decapitation and the splitting open of the breast: the standard masonic oath had the mason swear to secrecy "under no less penalty, than to have my throat cut, my tongue taken from the roof of my mouth, my heart plucked from under my left breast . . ."[116] It is curious to note that Rashid Rida in his voluminous biography is utterly silent on the details of this trial.

While 'Abduh was in Egypt trying to negotiate the rapids of *coup d'état* and rebellion and finally meeting with disaster, his master found himself in Hyderabad. An Indian informant of the Resident said he stayed in the town engaging in philosophical discussion and teaching. According to the files of the Indian C.I.D., his companions at that time were "the rising generation of freethinkers, the followers of Sayad Ahmed of Aligarh".

Afghani and 'Abduh

In her paper, previously cited, Professor Keddie makes the sound point that there seems to be little real difference between Afghani's doctrines and those of Sayyid Ahmad whom he so savagely attacked in his *Refutation of the Materialists*, and that Afghani objected more to Sayyid Ahmad's anglophilia than to his heterodoxy.* The point seems to be confirmed and emphasised by Afghani's associations in Hyderabad. His presence must have been unwelcome to the Nizam's government, for according to this informant, the Nizam's Minister gave him some 2,000 rupees to induce him to go away, but he stayed on nonetheless until the Egyptian crisis broke out in 1882, when he was said to have gone to Burma but, thought the informant, really to Egypt or to Paris.[117]

Afghani next appears in Calcutta in the early part of 1882. "There", says the Indian C.I.D.'s memorandum, "he offered his services to Government, but they were declined with thanks".† As the world has seen ever since the French Revolution, an ideological style of politics is, contrary to the claims of its practitioners, no guarantee of upright and consequent political behaviour, and Afghani's offer to become a British agent need occasion no surprise. He was of course not alone in exhibiting such a remarkable gulf between professions and actions. To confine ourselves to Afghani's own associates, we have seen how Adib Ishaq became a propagandist for Sharif and Isma'il against Riad, and how his patron rewarded him with office. Adib's newspapers then became the mouthpiece of 'Urabi's movement, until his Christian origins aroused the enmity of 'Urabi's increasingly Muslim *entourage*. Adib then had to leave Egypt, and he became 'Urabi's enemy, attacking him in a poem—his only weapon—for his despotism and for the looting of Alexandria in which 'Urabi's troops, Adib proclaimed, were thieves in soldiers'

---

* A scurrilous attack on Sayyid Ahmad in *al-Urwa al-wuthqa*, no. 15 (28 August 1884) accuses him of preaching his materialist doctrine to curry favour with the British and to weaken the Muslims in India. It is significant that the article makes a distinction between Sayyid Ahmad and those who hold materialist doctrines in Europe; the latter are fervently patriotic while the former spread their teachings precisely in order to weaken oriental patriotism and facilitate the domination of the foreigner.

† In his letter to Riad previously cited (*Documents*, plates 34–7), Afghani has a cryptic passage which may be a confirmation of the C.I.D.'s report. He says that while in Calcutta he was exposed to such pressure by the government that in order to escape persecution he had asked them as a last resort "to send me to the Khedive". Did he offer to act as an agent in Egypt?

dress.[118] There was again Sanua, the scourge of despotism, who laboured to overthrow Isma'il and Taufiq, but zealously advanced the cause of their uncle Halim and, in his later years, of their suzerain Abdul Hamid.[119] Again there was Sabunji who, in the apt words of Blunt,

> "after many vicissitudes of fortune drifted to that common haven of Oriental revolutionists, Yildiz Kiosk, where he obtained the confidential post with Sultan Abdul Hamid of translator for the Sultan's private eye of the European Press".[120]

Last but not least there is 'Abduh's remarkable history; heterodox in religion, radical in politics, he takes part in a rebellion, collaborates in the writing of a subversive print, but in the end, breaking with Afghani and his past becomes, thanks to the prudential liberality of the English occupier and the liberalism of Sir Evelyn Baring, the eminent and respected Mufti and Member of the Legislative Council, his renown and influence outstripping by far the seedy intellectuals and conspirators among whom his career began.

The circumstances of 'Abduh's elevation are noteworthy. It was on Baring's advice[121] that he was allowed, in 1889, to return from his exile. He was appointed *qadi* in the religious courts, and afterwards a Judge of Appeal in the Native Courts—so-called, to distinguish them from the Mixed Tribunals. In 1899 the Judicial adviser, Mr. McIlwraith, prepared a scheme of reforms for the Muslim religious courts which tried to remedy long-standing abuses and to guard against corruption. The scheme was debated in the Legislative Council on 10 May, and defended in long and able speeches by Ministers and by the Judicial Adviser. But it encountered the determined opposition of the Grand Qadi, Shaikh Jamal al-Din, and of the Mufti of Egypt, who was at the same time Rector of al-Azhar, Shaikh Hassuna al-Nawawi; he, in particular, "rendered himself especially conspicuous" as Cromer put it in a despatch, "by the violence of his expressions and his discourteous attitude towards the Ministers".[122] What the Mufti and his colleagues particularly disliked was a provision that civil magistrates could be appointed to sit with a *qadi* in a religious court. Civil magistrates, explained the Mufti, had to enforce a Code which recognised as legitimate the levying of interest, something which the *shari'a* forbade. The measure was unanimously rejected by the unofficial Muslim members of the Legislative Council. But the Government proceeded nonetheless to promulgate the decree of reform—as it had the power to do, and the decree, dated 15 May, appeared in the Official Gazette of 18 May.[123] But this reform aroused "so much opposition among the Moslem population that it has been thought desirable", wrote Cromer, "not to insist on its immediate execution". It appears from a letter of Cromer's to Salisbury commenting on the incident that it was the result of McIlwraith's zeal:

> "My Judicial Adviser", he wrote, "who is full of good intentions, but Scotch and unimaginative, has got me into trouble with the religious lights of the Moslem world in connection with certain reforms. He acted in full agreement with the Khedive and his Ministers. Unfortunately neither the Khedive nor his Ministers know anything of Mohammedan public opinion. This seems strange, but I have no doubt of the fact. Having got into the mess," he concluded, "I must, of course, back him up and come off victorious".[124]

And it was on Cromer's own advice, as we learn from his annual report for 1899[125] that the decree of reform was not brought into operation. We may take it that it was equally on his advice—in order that he might, after all, come off victorious—that the Government proceeded to deal with those who had so temerariously thwarted their enlightened and liberal benevolence. A Khedivial decree of 3 June forthwith dismissed Shaikh Hassuna al-Nawawi from his position as Rector of al-Azhar and Mufti of Egypt. To the first position Shaikh 'Abd al-Rahman al-Qutb al-Nawawi was appointed, and to the second Shaikh Muhammad 'Abduh. The Grand Qadi, owing his appointment to the Ottoman Sultan, could not be touched. Informing his Government that "the principal opponent of the proposed change has been removed from his place", Cromer went on to say that his successor "is believed to be animated with liberal sentiments and it is hoped that he will aid in the course of reform".[126] The rebel of the eighteen-seventies, the subversive journalist of the eighteen-eighties, was thus indebted for his exalted position to the despotism of the Khedivial Government which the British occupant was endeavouring to tincture with some benevolence. It remains to add that successive annual reports by the Judicial Adviser and by the British Resident and Consul-General from 'Abduh's appointment until his death record with unfailing regularity the absolute failure to effect any substantial reform in the religious courts. 'Abduh's appointment thus added one more link to the long chain by which the Muslim Institution was shackled into utter subservience to the Ruling Institution. On this episode Rashid Rida is again utterly silent in his biography, and the spirited Shaikh Hassuna is now quite forgotten.

Afghani's offer to the British authorities in Calcutta was repeated certainly to two and possibly three other powers. What the British spurned, others took up. Can this be the reason for Afghani's Anglophobia which, after that date, became strident and systematic? After Calcutta, at any rate, we find him in Paris writing anti-British tracts. One of these he sent to his Hyderabad acquaintance, Syed Hussein, and it was on its receipt that the latter was moved to write to the Resident. Syed Hussein had an interesting suggestion to make:

"I may add", he wrote to the Resident, "that to my knowledge the man is penniless, and must therefore have some kind of support at Paris. Whether he is or is not countenanced by the French government it is not for me to say, perhaps the strained relations between France and England may account for his existence at Paris."

It is a shrewd surmise worthy of serious consideration since, as a matter of fact, *al-Urwa al-wuthqa* was, as its editors stated,[127] given away free. Who then financed it? The attitude of the French government to British enquiries about Afghani again gives food for thought. In 1883 Afghani aroused the interest of the Foreign Office, because they suspected him or people connected with him of sending anonymous threatening letters to prominent persons in Egypt both British and Egyptian including Sharif and Sir Evelyn Baring. They asked the British Ambassador to find out from the French Foreign Ministry whether anything was known about him. Lord Lyons, in reply, doubted whether, the French being so irritated with the course of events in Egypt, any information would be forthcoming, "and it would not, I think," he added, "be politic to raise a question of the kind with them at this time". The Foreign Office still wanting the information, they got the C.I.D. to write to the Préfecture de Police, who replied that Afghani was known to them as an "homme de lettres", that he seemed to be in easy financial circumstances, and that neither his habitual conduct nor his morals gave rise to suspicion.[128] Whether the French police really knew no more, or whether they would not divulge what they knew, remains a moot point, which material in the French archives may in due course settle. It is, at any rate, reasonable to presume that having offered his services to the British, Afghani would offer them again to the French;

it is also legitimate to assume that anti-British propaganda directed to Egypt would not have been unwelcome to the French at that period. But this, of course, remains a speculation, to which however his connexions with Khalil Ghanim and the newspaper *al-Basir* lend some support. This newspaper and *al-Urwa al-wuthqa* were printed by the same firm, edited from the same address, and shared the same *gérant*, which may be a coincidence, but again may not.

It was *al-Basir* which in its issue of 27 January 1883 announced in fulsome terms the arrival in Paris for an extended stay of "the man of action and science, of the perfect philosopher" (*al-'allama al-'amil wa'l failasuf al-kamil*), Sayyid Jamal al-Din. *Al-Basir* was an Arabic newspaper which began to be published with official support in April, 1881, when Franco-Tunisian relations were reaching a critical stage, and it concentrated, to start with, on answering Italian propaganda among the Tunisians. Its first editor was a Lebanese Christian, Yusuf Bakhos, who had in fact been editing a similar sheet for the Italians and who had been induced to desert his first employers and take employment with their rivals. But there is little doubt that *al-Basir* was in effect directed by Khalil Ghanim, who at first, however, denied for some reason all connexion with it, but who from no. 43 onwards, advertised himself as its proprietor and political director. Khalil Ghanim, a Maronite, had been Dragoman for the Vali of Syria, then for the Grand Vizierate in Istanbul, and finally a member of the first Ottoman parliament representing Syria.[129] When 'Abd al-Hamid disbanded this assembly in 1879, Khalil Ghanim went to Paris where, it is clear, he was employed by the French Government. He was given French citizenship and awarded the *Légion d'honneur*. When he assumed responsibility openly for *al-Basir*, he printed a notice in French which appeared in several issues and was addressed "*Aux Français d'Orient*", asking for their collaboration in distributing his newspaper, the aim of which, he said, was "*apprendre enfin aux arabes à aimer la France.*" After the British occupation of Egypt, *al-Basir*, taking its cue from French policy, was at once anti-British and anti-Ottoman. Anti-British, because the French Government was furious with the British for having occupied Egypt on their own, and anti-Ottoman because the French suspected the Sultan of spreading panislamic propaganda in North Africa. The columns of this newspaper were opened to Afghani who, published there several anti-British articles.[130]

Afghani and 'Abduh 41

Khalil Ghanim also wrote for the *Journal des Débats*, with which Renan was connected. It was he, Renan tells us, who introduced Afghani to him.[131] And the *Journal des Débats* was among the first of European newspapers to announce Afghani's presence in Paris. Its number of 6 April, 1883, gives extracts from an article which Afghani had written shortly before for a periodical edited by Georges Clémenceau, *La Justice*, attacking British designs on the Muslims and imputing to them the desire—of which Russia and France were innocent—to make Christian proselytes in the Muslim world.[132] These extracts were prefaced by a passage giving details of Afghani's history. There is little doubt that the writer was Khalil Ghanim, and equally little doubt that the details were supplied by Afghani. Afghani, the newspaper said, was born in Kabul "of a princely family" in 1848, had taken part in Afghan politics in support of Afdal Khan, had fled to India and had then gone to Istanbul. He was there "authorised by the Sultan" to lecture on religious subjects in Santa Sophia and in the mosque of Sultan Ahmad, and roused the *'ulama*

"by reason of the liberal doctrines which he taught and which were stamped with that Greek philosophy which, as M. Renan has shown, was so greatly honoured among the Iranians and their neighbours".

We thus see that Afghani had no objection to being presented to a European audience as an "enlightened" thinker attacking Muslim obscurantism. This of course is the very posture which he adopts in his well-known commentary—wrongly called an answer or a refutation—on Renan's lecture, *Islam and Science*, which appeared in the *Journal des Débats* of 18 May[133] and where, as Renan immediately recognised, Afghani in effect improved on the original argument by insisting that not only Islam but all other revealed religions were equally reactionary and obscurantist. Afghani seems to have written his comments in Arabic and, when publishing them, the newspaper explained that it was giving "as faithful a translation as possible". It can, of course, be objected that faithful as the translation was claimed to be, it might yet have misrepresented Afghani. This is certainly a point to bear in mind, but it must be recognised that the weight of the evidence tells against it.

In the first place, let us note that Afghani had one curious comment to make on Renan's lecture. When the lecture was published, a Frenchman in Algeria wrote to *al-Basir* protesting that its aspersions on Islam might damage French interests in

Islamic countries, and pointing out that Renan's condemnation of Islam as obscurantist was by no means universally accepted. This letter drew from Afghani a note contrasting French and British behaviour. Here is Renan, he said, making a perfectly civil speech and not once wounding the feelings of the Muslims; yet even so, a Frenchman objects and takes it upon himself to defend Islam. Compare this noble behaviour with the practice of the English in India who force Protestantism on the Muslims and persecute those *'ulama* who dare to argue with the missionaries.[134] This language hardly shows that Afghani objected to Renan's original arguments. But what particularly tells against this point is what Renan had to say about Afghani's observations. In his comment, which appeared on 19 May, Renan declared that it was his conversations with Afghani—whom he described as an *Asiatique éclairé*—which decided him to lecture on Islam and science; he went on:

"Shaikh Jamal al-Din is an Afghan entirely liberated from the prejudices of Islam; he belongs to those active races of upper Iran, on the confines of India, where the Aryan spirit still actively survives under the superficial veneer of official Islam. He is the best proof of the great axiom which we have often proclaimed, namely that the value of a religion is proportionate to the worth of the race which professes it. The freedom of his thought, his noble and loyal character, gave me the impression, while talking to him, that I had in front of me one of my ancient acquaintances, such as Avicenna or Averroes, or some other one of those great unbelievers who, for five centuries, upheld the tradition of the human spirit."[135]

It is difficult to believe that Renan was so fanciful, or that the interpreter was so ignorant, that Afghani's views—which were enough for Renan to describe him as "a great unbeliever"—were completely distorted in the transmission. In any case, Afghani, so far as is known, never protested against the ascription to him of views which, had he been an orthodox Muslim, he would have considered damaging and offensive. In fact, the only other reference in the *Moscow Gazette* article mentioned above, apart from Vauquelin, which Afghani thought worth giving to his Russian audience, was precisely this article of Renan's which, the *Gazette* stated, "gives an account of an interview with the Sheikh".

Ernest Renan, as has been seen, believed that his lecture on *Islam and Science* was inspired by his conversations with Afghani.

Delivered at the Sorbonne on 29 March 1883, the lecture constituted a eulogy of Hellenism as the source of science and progress in Europe, and an outspoken attack on Islam as an engine of despotism, terror and persecution. Islam, in his view, was an invention of the Arab nomads who destroyed the high civilization of the Sasanids and the Byzantines. To start with, Islam was not able completely to do away with science and learning in the conquered regions, but eventually its theological deadhand stifled and killed all free thought and all philosophical speculation. "The liberals who defend Islam", he said, "do not know it. Islam is the complete unity of the spiritual and the temporal, it is the reign of a dogma, it constitutes the heaviest chains which have ever shackled humanity. In the first half of the Middle Ages . . . Islam put up with philosophy, because it could not do away with it; it could not do away with it, because it lacked cohesion and was little equipped to use terror. . . . But when Islam found that it could depend on masses of ardent believers, then it destroyed everything. Religious terror and hypocrisy were the order of the day. Islam was liberal", Renan affirmed, "when it was weak, and violent when it was strong." Islam, he was firmly convinced, had done nothing but harm to human reason; it had persecuted free thought, "I will not say more violently than other religious systems, but more efficiently. Those countries which it conquered, it shut off against the rational culture of the spirit."

It is on an attack of this kind, couched in these harsh and uncompromising terms, that Afghani chose to make a public comment. And the comment in effect amounted to an endorsement of Renan's condemnation. Afghani makes no secret here of his belief that religion has been on the whole a force for evil in human history. In the infancy of the race, when the human mind was swayed by nameless terrors, and was incapable of distinguishing good from evil, religion had no doubt proved to have some use. At that time the educators of the race had been compelled to enforce obedience to their necessary rules and orders by ascribing them to a Supreme Being. It was, said Afghani, "a most heavy and humiliating yoke", but it was the price which had to be paid for escape from barbarism. All religions, asserts Afghani, are intolerant. Islam did seek to stifle science and to arrest intellectual freedom, but so did Christianity—and this is almost the only point at which he takes issue with Renan, objecting that his attack on Islam should be widened to include all religions. But Afghani does not in the least hesitate to agree that Islam has been for many centuries fanatical and obscurantist: "Wherever it has established itself", he affirms, "this religion has tried to stifle science and it has been marvellously served in its aims by despotism." Afghani's conclusion is worth quoting at length: "Religions", he wrote, "by whatever name they are called, resemble one another. No understanding and no reconciliation is possible between these religions and philosophy. Religion imposes its faith and its creed on man, while philosophy liberates him from them wholly or in part. How then can people wish for an understanding between them? When the Christian religion under the most modest and seductive forms entered Athens and Alexandria which were, as everyone knows, the two principal centres of science and philosophy, its first care after having been firmly established was to push on one side science properly so-called and philosophy, by attempting to stifle the one and the other in the undergrowth of theological discussions meant to explain the inexplicable mysteries of the Trinity, of the Incarnation and of Transsubstantiation. It will always be so. Every time that religion has the upper hand, it will eliminate philosophy; and the contrary takes place when it is philosophy which rules as a sovereign mistress. So long as humanity subsists, the struggle will not cease between dogma and free enquiry, between religion and philosophy, a bitter struggle from which, I fear, free thought will not emerge victorious, because reason does not please the mass and its teachings are understood only by a few choice spirits, and also because science, however beautiful it is, cannot completely satisfy humanity which is athirst for an ideal which it likes to place in obscure and distant regions which philosophers and men of science can neither glimpse nor explore."

It is of some interest to follow the fortunes in the East of the exchange between Renan and Afghani. A letter from 'Abduh in Beirut to Afghani in Paris dated 8 Sha'ban 1300 and reproduced in the *Documents*[136] is of extreme importance in shedding light not only on this matter but on the nature of Afghani's esoteric teaching. The letter begins with those expressions of idolatry of which I have given in Appendix I a characteristic specimen. Then 'Abduh goes on to say that news had reached him of Afghani's answer to Renan in the *Journal des Débats;* he had thought that a translation would serve to edify the believers and had asked a man of religion (*ba'd al-diniyyin*) to be ready to undertake it on receipt of the French text. But immediately afterwards, 'Abduh

writes, he received two numbers of the *Journal* (presumably of 18 and 19 May 1883, containing Afghani's commentary and Renan's observations), together with a letter from Afghani. He goes on:
> "We then praised Almighty God that the numbers of the *Débats* had not been available before the receipt of your letter. We acquainted ourselves with these two numbers which Hasan effendi Bayhum translated for us. We then dissuaded our first friend from making the translation, alleging that Arabic text was going to be sent, that it would be published then, and that therefore there was no need for a translation. Thus misfortune was averted (*fa'ndafa'a al-makruh*), God be praised."

Since Afghani's commentary was a powerful attack on traditional Islam, it is not surprising that neither Afghani nor 'Abduh desired its dissemination in Islamic countries. But the sentences which immediately follow are even more significant:
> "We regulate our conduct", writes 'Abduh, "according to your sound rule: we do not cut the head of religion except with the sword of religion (*nahnu al-an 'ala sunnatika al-qawima la naqta'** *ra's al-din illa bi-saif al-din*). Therefore, if you were to see us now, you would see ascetics and worshippers [of God] kneeling and genuflecting, never disobeying what God commands and doing all that they are ordered to do. Ah! how constricted life would be without hope!"

This letter makes absolutely clear that one of Afghani's aims— of which his disciple 'Abduh knew and approved—was the subversion of the Islamic religion, and that the method adopted to this end was the practice of a false but showy devotion.

In fact, Afghani's comment on Renan's lecture does not seem to have been at all translated into Arabic.[137] In his article on Afghani in the first edition of the *Encyclopædia of Islam*, I. Goldziher stated that Renan's lecture was translated into Arabic and published with a rejoinder by Hasan Asim. This translation I have not been able to see. In 1923, the Egyptian University at Cairo organised a celebration in honour of Renan's memory, and Shaikh Mustafa Abd al-Raziq delivered a lecture on the exchange between Renan and Afghani in which he seems to have taken the

---
* An alternative reading would be, *la taqta'*: do not cut.

view—so Rashid Rida reported—that after his arrival in Paris in 1883 Afghani suffered a change in belief,

"became a rebel against religion, and came to believe that it was the enemy of science, reason and civilization, so much so that he gladly and deferentially acquiesced in Renan's attack on Islam."[138]

In making these statements, Mustafa Abd al-Raziq was, if anything, greatly underestimating the period when Afghani was alienated from Islam, but his lecture gave great offence to Rashid Rida, who accused him of basing his remarks merely on a German translation of the French text.[139] In an undated letter which must have been written after these events, he asks his friend Shakib Arslan to provide him with a translation of Afghani's remarks on Renan's lecture and adds, "Shaikh Mustafa Abd al-Raziq and his friends have searched for but have not been able to find it".[140] From a letter of 12 May, 1924, we gather that Shakib Arslan had not provided his friend with the translation, but merely with extracts from Goldziher's article in the *Encyclopædia of Islam*; in this letter Shakib insisted on the probable unreliability of the translator who had rendered Afghani's text into French and on the anti-Muslim prejudices of the *Journal des Débats*.[141] Shakib Arslan could read French, and may well have known the exact tenor of Afghani's argument; but he may have judged it more discreet and more politic to refrain from providing a text which would have discomforted his friend and shaken Afghani's reputation.

Apart from Vauquelin and Khalil Ghanim, Afghani knew another Parisian journalist, namely Henri Rochefort, the editor of *L'Intransigeant*, who, in fact, devotes some pages to him in his autobiography.[142] Rochefort states that he came to know Afghani through some Egyptian officers who had taken refuge in France after the collapse of 'Urabi's movement; Vauquelin he does not mention. One of Afghani's striking qualities is the intuitive grasp he seems to have of the nature of the political power to be gained by mastering and manipulating the masses, and of the requisite demagogic arts. Rochefort's testimony in this respect—the testimony of an admirer—is all the more valuable in that Rochefort accepted Afghani's professions at their face value, and can have had no inkling of the character's involuted subtlety or the tortuosities of his career. Rochefort describes Afghani as "*le type du dominateur des foules*", and goes on:

"He [Afghani] used to say to me with his Asiatic subtlety, 'England had thought it a great act of policy to impose the English language on the Hindus, whether Muslims or idolators, but she has made a tremendous mistake. Today they understand the newspapers which their conquerors publish and realise perfectly well the state of subjection to which they have been reduced'."

To appreciate literacy as a political weapon is a first necessity for the modern demagogue. Afghani did appreciate it, for, as we learn from Rochefort,

"it was by the bale that he himself would send pamphlets and newspaper extracts to the most obscure townships where he had long lived, which developed in them the spirit of insurrection."

Whether Afghani's literary exports were as large as he allowed Rochefort to believe, we do not know, but if they were, it becomes even more interesting to penetrate the mystery of his finances.

Rochefort, in his innocence, recounts another story which throws light on another characteristic of Afghani's, his love, namely, of boastfulness and self-glorification. Afghani's sojourn in Paris coincided with the irruption of the Sudanese Mahdi onto the newspaper headlines. Afghani not only claimed that the Mahdi, who had never left the Sudan, had been a pupil of his at al-Azhar in Cairo (where Afghani hardly taught), but he professed to be able, by means of letters of introduction, to smooth the path of a French journalist, Olivier Pain, who sympathised with the Mahdi and wanted to penetrate into Mahdist territory and thus make a great journalistic scoop. Pain set out, armed with Afghani's missives, and succeeded in reaching El Obeid in August 1884. He was not received with open arms, as he had clearly expected, but was imprisoned as a spy, and the more he proclaimed his sympathy for Mahdism the more suspect he seemed. Shortly afterwards he succumbed to ill-treatment and disease; as he was being transported on a camel

"he was seized with a fainting fit, and fell off. As he lay unconscious on the ground, and was deathly pale, his guards believed that he must be dead; so they dug a rough grave, in which poor Pain was laid, covered him over with sand, and then hurried on. It is quite possible the unfortunate man was not dead. They marked his grave by planting his stick in the sand, and tying his sandals to it. This event occurred on the 15th November, 1884."[143]

Afghani, as we know, instigated Shah Nasir al-Din's murder, but that at least was to gratify his lust for vengeance and indulge his political passions; it was to satisfy a more frivolous craving that he helped to send the foolish and trusting Pain to his miserable end.

Rochefort's newspaper, *L'Intransigeant*, published two articles by Afghani. The first, on 24 April, 1883, was entitled "Lettre sur L'Hindoustan"; it is an attack on British rule in India, and a confident expectation of an insurrection brought about by the oppression they practised.[144] The second one was published over three issues, on 8, 11 and 17 December, 1883. It is entitled "Le Mahdi" and was obviously occasioned by the destruction which the Hicks expedition had just suffered at the hands of the Sudanese Mahdi.* In introducing the first and second parts the newspaper emphasised that the article was published exactly as it was received. This article throws a particularly clear light on Afghani's political ideas and neatly exhibits the esoteric element in his teaching.

The idea of a *mahdi* in Islam is messianic and apocalyptic. Whether in Shi'ite doctrine or Sunni sentiment, the *mahdi* is a saviour who comes to establish justice, banish iniquity, and restore the reign of divine law. In Shi'ite theology, of which the mahdist idea is an essential part, this saviour is the withdrawn *imam* to whom alone, as a descendant of Ali, rule by divine right legitimately belongs, and who will, at the end of time, manifest himself with signs and prodigies. Among the Sunnis, the idea of a *mahdi* is far from central; as Goldziher points out, it has never become accepted as a dogma; "it never appears but as the mythological ornament of an ideal future, as an accessory to the system which follows from the orthodox conception of the universe."[145] In the Sunni view, the *mahdi*, descendant of the Prophet as he is, is yet no charismatic saviour but an ordinary man who comes as a reformer and conqueror, a caliph supremely well-guided restoring Islam to its pristine simplicity and morning glory.[146]

But whatever their varying conceptions, both Shi'ites and Sunnis are agreed that the *mahdi*, if he is anything, is a religious leader, that his coming heralds the renewal of the religious life in an Islamic community henceforth entirely guided by the precepts of the *shari'a*. This certainly is the burden of the Sudanese Mahdi's

*See Appendix II for the text of these articles.

preaching; he is a warner denouncing the corruption of the age and calling for a devout and holy life.[147]

It is very significant that in Afghani's article the fundamental religious character and purpose of the *mahdi* is little noticed, that in fact it is as a secular political leader rather than a religious saviour that he is exhibited. In the first part of this article, where Afghani begins by giving an account of the traditional notion of the *mahdi* in Islam (which has some interesting pecularities), he does say that the *mahdi's* "divine mission" is to suppress undesirable innovations in religion and propagate Islam all over the world. But what he does stress throughout the rest of his article is that the hallmark of the *mahdi* is purely military success. Thus in the first part he writes:

"Briefly, how many Muslim personalities have, under this appellation, accomplished striking and tremendous actions and have brought about far-reaching changes in the world of believers"; again in the same part he says: "Finally, the prestige of the Mahdi in the eyes of the Muslims will solely depend on the ultimate success which he will be able to obtain".

In the second part of his article, he explains that

"he who rises in the name of religion, proclaiming himself prophet or *mahdi*, can never abandon his course, convinced as he is that if he retreats, the confidence which his followers have in him will begin to weaken and will surely end by disappearing", and he adds: "The motto of a *mahdi*, therefore, can be nothing but this: either to die or to reach his goal."

We may say that almost the only point at which Afghani's conception is identical with the traditional one lies in the fact that for both the *mahdi* is a man of the sword, *sahib al-saif*, as he is called in Shi'ite literature.[148] But whereas for traditional Islam it is only one of the signs of a *mahdi* that he comes with a sword, for Afghani the *mahdi* is a *mahdi* only because he knows how to wield the sword.

In fact, Afghani's vision is that of a secular apocalypse and his creed is a political messianism. We may see this clearly if we examine the way in which he presents *mahdism* to the readers of *L'Intransigeant*. As has been seen, belief in the *mahdi* is an essential part of the Shi'ite creed, and it may well be that Afghani's Shi'ite upbringing lies at the origin of his clear predilection for mahdism. What does transpire from his article is that he is totally indifferent to the specific details of the Shi'ite belief: he reports baldly the

Shi'ite expectation of a *mahdi* descended from Ali as he reports various other forms of this belief held by other Muslim sects; there is, he says in the first part of his article, such a profusion of of diverse detail in the numerous prophecies concerning the coming of the *mahdi*, that it is profitless to recount them; again he says, in the same part, however various the "forms" of such a belief, the fact remains that every Muslim awaits a *mahdi*. The impression we get from his language here is of a sceptic surveying the infinity of human superstition and error.

But he is not quite the sceptic; for behind the "forms" which he so casually dismisses, Afghani seems to believe that there is an essence, so to speak, which represents what is valid and true in *mahdist* beliefs. What this is may best be described in his own words. He begins his article by stating that his object will be to explain what Islam expects from the *mahdi*. He then goes on to assert that the belief in the coming of a *mahdi* is rooted in the Islamic peoples since the first century of the *hijra*, that this belief is based on

> "innumerable and very respected sayings attributed to the great prophet Muhammad", that all Muslim divines, "except Ibn Khaldun, and a few others the number of whom is very limited", have "unanimously" recognised the authenticity of these sayings.

Afghani quotes some of the sayings which appear in the treatises and adds that other sayings of the same kind

> "prove in a no less clear fashion the certain belief that a *mahdi* will come". Afghani also says in the same part that "the expectation of a *mahdi* is so intensified among Muslims every time they find themselves in difficulties, or their religion threatened or a foreign power dominating them, that they then resemble a man lost on a dark night in a vast desert awaiting with impatience the appearance of a star which might guide him."

And, as has been mentioned above, having dismissed the exact "form" of a belief in the *mahdi* as of no importance, he concludes the first part of his article by saying that

> "it is nonetheless true that every Muslim awaits a *mahdi* for whom he is ready to sacrifice his life and all his possessions. The Indian Muslims in particular, in view of their infinite sufferings and the cruel torments they undergo under English domination, await him with the greatest impatience."

It is clear that Afghani, under cover of expounding the Muslim creed, is in fact describing his own grandiose soteriological vision of an all-powerful leader followed by a vast mass of Muslims who, by their belief in him, would gain the strength to rise against and annihilate their foreign oppressors. The difference between his conception of the *mahdi* and that, say of Muhammad Ahmad, the actual Sudanese Mahdi, is brought out by a sentence which occurs in the last paragraph of the second part of his article where he speaks of the Indian Muslims considering the Sudanese Mahdi to be their "saviour". The reason why they do so, Afghani clearly thinks, is because Muhammad Ahmad is waging successful war against their British oppressors. How removed this is from the traditional views of the actual Mahdi who believed that the true purpose of his mission was to restore religion, and that success in war merely confirmed that his call was divinely inspired!

The second part of Afghani's article exhibits his doctrine with great clarity. Does England hope, he asks,

"to stifle the voice of the Mahdi, the most awesome of all voices since its power is even greater than the voice of the Holy War, which issues from all Muslim mouths?" "Does she think herself able," he goes on, "to stifle this voice before making itself heard in all the East from Mount Himalaya to Dawlaghir, from north to south, speaking to the Muslims of Afghanistan, of Sind and of India, proudly proclaiming the coming of the Saviour whom every son of Islam awaits with such impatience. *El-Mahdi, El-Mahdi, El-Mahdi!*" Finally in the last part of his article, Afghani declares that "all Muslims await the *mahdi* and consider his coming as an absolute necessity."

It is clear, then, that Afghani's view of the *mahdi* owes a great deal to the Shi'ite expectation of a superhuman saviour at the end of time. It is equally clear that the original Shi'ite idea has, in his case, left its religious moorings and become the plaything of a romantic imagination intoxicated by a glimpse of the immense power which anyone might capture who knew how to evoke the blind obedience of the masses and tend the fires of their devotion. One sees him computing possibilities and considering the ways and means.

"Man," he remarks in the last part of his article, "is by nature given to exaggerating all news which comes to him from afar, so that the figure *one* travelling from one mouth to another and augmented by public rumour soon ends up by becoming the figure *thousand;* the hillock comes to be considered a mountain. This is why, at the announcement of the coming of a *mahdi*, the hearts of all those who are waiting for their liberation will be filled with great expectations and will overflow with joy and hope."

An armed and veiled prophet, with rumour as his agent and myth his weapon, this seems to be his ideal of political action; it is not fanciful to see here the explanation of Afghani's sustained and sedulous propagation of so many legends about himself.

A man who avows such a belief in the power of rumour may easily be suspected of spreading nothing but baseless rumours. How much of what Afghani says can be believed? For him speech more frequently serves to persuade and deceive, but it is clear that on occasion we may take him to be speaking the truth. It is clear, for instance, that when 'Abduh writes to him that "we are still following your sound rule: we do not cut the head of religion except with the sword of religion," he is disclosing something of Afghani's most esoteric teaching reserved for the most intimate of his disciples. Again, his anxiety that his exchange with Renan should not be known in Islamic countries indicates that here is something to which he attached some value, since in disclosing it to Renan, he took the risk that it might go beyond Renan and his European audience. Similarly in his article on "The Mahdi" published in a French socialist newspaper he had no reason to go beyond denunciations of British imperialism (which the article does contain in good measure) and embark on this peculiar exposition of mahdism unless he felt the need to unburden himself safely of convictions which lay close to his heart. That these views on the *mahdi* constitute for Afghani an esoteric teaching not safely to be spread *urbi et orbi* is indicated by the contrast between the *Intransigeant* article and the treatment of mahdism in his Arabic writings.

In the second part of his article Afghani discusses *mahdi* and caliph. He states:

"The Muslims believe in fact that the Caliphate, whether legitimate, i.e. in the hands of a Quraishi—a member of Muhammad's tribe—or illegitimate, i.e. in the hands of a conqueror, must disappear at the manifestation of the *mahdi*, who would himself be the true Caliph of the believers."

By Muslims in this passage Afghani must be taken to mean Sunnis, since Shi'ites have never acknowledged a Caliph, legitimate

Afghani and 'Abduh

or illegitimate, except the Hidden Imam who is held to be still alive and who will appear at the appointed time. We may notice in passing the way in which Afghani attributes a belief indiscriminately to all Muslims, and may take this as an indication that he is concerned not so much to expound the creed as to use an expository mode for investing his particular views with a spurious authority. If Afghani's statement then is to make sense, for Muslims we must read Sunnis, and what he is then seen to be asserting is that a *mahdi*, immediately he declares himself, has the primacy over a reigning Caliph. This is obviously a revolutionary and subversive doctrine; is it, nonetheless, accepted Sunni doctrine? It is nothing of the kind. Sunni doctors have accepted as authentic a saying attributed to the Prophet which runs:

"There will be Caliphs after me, and after the Caliphs princes, and after the princes kings, and after the kings tyrants (*jababira*), and then a man from my house will appear who will fill the earth with justice as it has been filled with injustice".[149]

In Sunni doctrine, then, the *mahdi* cannot appear when there is a Caliph; he only appears at a time of disorder and arbitrariness when legitimate and stable authority has disappeared. This argument in fact was one of those used by the religious doctors in Egypt and the Sudan in order to denounce Muhammad Ahmad as an impostor: this man, they argued, cannot be the *mahdi*, since a legitimate Caliph exists whose right to rule has not been questioned.[150] We must also note that the Ottoman authorities themselves considered the Sudanese Mahdi a threat to the Caliphate and went to the trouble of disseminating manifestos in Muslim countries denouncing his pretentions.[151] In fact the traditional and long-standing attitude of the Ottoman Caliphate to mahdism is one of consistent and uncompromising hostility. The treatise of the Hanafi shaikh Ibrahim al-Halabi (d. 1549), *Multaqa al-abhur*, which authoritatively sums up orthodox teaching and jurisprudence as transmitted in the Empire, states: "The Imam must be visible; he must neither hide from the eyes of the public, nor be the object of its [messianic] expectation."[152] All this leaves no doubt that from a Sunni point of view Afghani's assertions of the primacy of *mahdi* over caliph is heterodox.

Afghani of course had no duty to follow Sunni orthodoxy, and if he had not at that very time set up as a champion of the Ottoman Caliphate there would have been little point in contrasting his views with the teachings of the Sunna. But, in fact, at the time of his *Intransigeant* article and later his public stance was that of a fervent defender of the Ottoman Caliphate. One of his first articles in Arabic after his arrival in Paris was an open letter to Khalil Ghanim published in *al-Basir* asking him not to be so harsh in attacking the Ottoman Empire;[153] whilst some two years later he instigated the Egyptian Ibrahim al-Muwailihi to write a memorial to Abdul Hamid in which he reported Afghani's readiness to use his good offices in solving the Sudanese question in a way acceptable to the Sultan.[154] But the evidence yielded by his famous newspaper *al-Urwa al-wuthqa* is the most significant and most revealing of all. A large number of articles in *al-Urwa* are concerned with Mahdism and the Sudan, and if we examine them, we will not only fail to discover a trace of the doctrine expounded in *L'Intransigeant*, we will actually find its opposite. Thus in an article entitled *"Nasiha"* ("A Piece of Advice"), it is stated:

"I fear as all wise men fear that the dissemination of this doctrine [mahdism] and the increase of its votaries will harm England and anyone having rights in Egypt. The English, therefore, as we have frequently advised them to do, must preserve their country and safeguard the route to India by delegating the matter [the Sudan] to the Ottomans and to those who have resolution among the Egyptians, before it is too late";

in an article entitled *"Inghilterra fi sawahil al-bahr al-ahmar"*, ("England on the shores of the Red Sea"), he refers to British defeats in the Sudan and conveys by his language the impression that the Mahdi's movement is unwelcome to him, thus:

"... it may be that the simple-minded (*al-sudhaj*) will be led by their illusions to believe that God has given them [the Mahdi's following] support by means of angels...";

in an article entitled *"Amal Inghilterra fi harakat Muhammad Ahmad* ("England's hopes in Muhammad Ahmad's operations"), he writes of the Mahdi:

"... whether he is truthful or lying in his preaching ... whether God will help him to succeed, or whether he will be the victim of ill-success, we have no wish to discuss now";

again, in the same article he asserts: "the strength of an Islamic preaching cannot be met except by an Islamic resolution; and none but Muslim men can struggle with this pretender (*mudda'i*) and reduce him to his proper stature";

finally, in an article entitled *"Turkiya"* (Turkey) he explains that the Mahdi arose only because Britain had occupied Egypt and that he would never have initiated his movement if the Sudan had still been under undivided Egyptian rule; he then goes on to exhort the Ottoman Empire to consider the danger of the Mahdi's movement spreading to India, Beluchistan and Afghanistan, to appreciate English weakness, the policies of the other Powers and then

> "show a stable resolution and strong courage as befits a great state such as the state of the house of 'Uthman, at whose hands extraordinary things have not seldom been accomplished."[155]

Al-Urwa was published for a space of eight months from May, 1884, when the Sudanese Mahdi was at the apogee of his power. Afghani's language here cannot therefore be ascribed to a change in political circumstances. We can say more. Even after the death of the Mahdi, he was still maintaining in private his partiality for him:

> "A long talk with Jamal ed-Din about the prospects at Constantinople and about the Caliphate," records Blunt on 8 October, 1885, "He is for the Mahdi or the Mahdi's successor taking the Sultan's place . . ."[156]

Does not the only consistent explanation of the remarkable difference between what Afghani says in French and what he says in Arabic lie in his lifelong distinction between what may safely be divulged to the vulgar and what may not be disclosed to them?

Afghani next appears in London in 1885 as Blunt's guest. The mission on which Sir Henry Drummond Wolff later went to Istanbul in order to negotiate an Egyptian settlement with the Sultan was then being considered, and Blunt tried very hard to get the British Government to invite Afghani to accompany Drummond Wolff, arguing that the Sayyid would mightily help British diplomacy; he had no success, and Afghani, offended, as Blunt thought, both with the British Government and with his host went away:

> "Jamal-ed-Din, who had been mysteriously absent for two or three days from James Street, turned up again this morning. He had left the house in consequence of a noisy disturbance that occurred in his room on Thursday between two of his Oriental friends, Wahbi Bey and Abd-el-Rasul; they seem to have quarrelled over politics or religion and ended by beating each other over the heads with umbrellas. I had to

beg them both to leave the house, and the Sayyid followed them. One must draw the line somewhere, and I have now suggested to the Sayyid that he should take up his quarters elsewhere; he has been three months with me in the house, the full term of Arab hospitality."[157]

It may be that Afghani took offence at the British thus spurning his advances for the second time, and that this, as Blunt suggests, governed his next move. Which, as a despatch from Baring of 23 October, 1886, informs us, was to go to Russia. An Indian judge had told him, he reported, that "the well-known Gellal Eddin" had gone to Petersburg "whither it is supposed he was invited by order of the Russian Government".[158] It may well be that Afghani's new connexion with Russia had nothing to do with his action in Afghanistan, for it is quite likely that the earlier venture had been encouraged not so much by the Russian Central Government as by its agents in Central Asia.[159] The biographical notices collected by Rashid Rida state that Afghani, in his period of his life, went to Persia twice, once in 1886 and again in 1889. His presence in Russia is at any rate recorded in 1887, 1888 and 1889. Whatever Afghani's relations with the French Government, there seems no doubt that he was a client and subsequently an agent of Russia. Afghani seems to have gone to Moscow at the invitation of the well-known Panslavist leader, Katkov, who was interested in organising anti-British agitation in Central Asia and India.[160] The *Moscow Gazette* of 1/13 July, 1887, published, as has been seen, an interview with Afghani in which he said that

> "his object in visiting Russia was to make himself practically acquainted with a country on which 60,000,000 Indian Mussulmans place sole reliance and which they hope will afford them protection and emancipate them from the detested English yoke."[161]

Katkov had enticed to Moscow another personage who also had a grudge against the British, and with whom Afghani collaborated in anti-British enterprises. This was Maharajah Dalip Singh (1838-1893), the last ruler of the Sikh Kingdom of the Punjab. The youngest son of Ranjit Singh, the famous Sikh leader, he was one year old when his father died. Internecine struggles among his brothers and among the Sikh leaders led to his brief period of rule, before his deposition by the British at Lahore in 1849. He was given a handsome pension and eventually settled on an estate in Suffolk, having embraced Christianity and married the daughter of an Abyssinian slave and a German banker whom he met in a

Presbyterian orphanage in Cairo.[162] In the mid-1880s, he started quarrelling with the India Office, demanding the restoration of his throne. He attempted to go to India, was stopped at Aden, where he renounced Christianity for the Sikh religion, came back to Paris, and, in 1887, patronised by Katkov, he turned up in Moscow announcing his plans for a Sikh rising and the speedy end of British rule in India. Afghani and Dalip Singh collaborated in issuing manifestos dated from Moscow signed, The Executive of the Indian Liberation Society, and printed and distributed with Fenian help in Paris.[163] Their activities may have extended further afield, for the threads of an intrigue concerning the Sudan were traced at Cairo, the man involved being the same Abd al-Rasul whose unseemly use of the umbrella had so shocked the hospitable Blunt.[164]

Katkov died in 1887, and this seems to have left both Afghani and Dalip Singh stranded. The latter, manifestly useless to the Russians, eventually returned to Paris. Afghani is reported in St. Petersburg in August, 1887, where, so the Ottoman Ambassador was informed, he was disappointed at the reception he had from the Russian officials who seem, except for the well-known Pobedonostsev, to have paid him no attention.[165] In 1888, the Indian C.I.D. had a report that he was at St. Petersburg where "he had impressed upon some Russian officials the prospects of a general rising in India whenever the Russians chose to give the signal."[166] Towards the end of 1889 he left Russia for Persia.

The standard sources—Rashid Rida, Makhzumi, Browne— state that Afghani went to Persia at the invitation of the Shah. The facts relating to Afghani's move seem, however, more complicated. In April, 1892, when Afghani was once more in London, mounting a campaign against the Shah, the Persian Minister to Russia told the British Ambassador that the Shah had given Afghani an audience in St. Petersburg in 1889, and invited him to visit Persia through the intercession of Amin al-Daulah.[167] If invitation there really was, the Shah seems to have quickly repented of it, for when Afghani did arrive in Tehran, the British Minister telegraphed that the Shah was annoyed at his arrival.[168] The Shah's annoyance was natural enough, for if he did not know while in St. Petersburg that Afghani was involved with the Russians, and hence possibly a Russian agent, there would have been no lack of people to enlighten him subsequently. Could an invitation or, what was more likely, a show of imperial benevolence which could be represented as an invitation, have been procured by subterfuge, by suppressing the fact of Afghani's connexion with the Russians? It is possible, and we must remember that Amin al-Daulah, who arranged the audience for Afghani, was the rival of Amin al-Sultan, then the Shah's Chief Minister,[169] and that he may have seen in Afghani a useful auxiliary in some future combination.

But was there ever an invitation, or anything which could be represented as such? Shortly after Afghani reached Tehran, rumours were heard that he was to be appointed Minister of the Press, and the British Legation enquired from Amin al-Sultan if this was true. The Minister said that he had not seen Afghani since his arrival at Tehran, that Afghani had written to him from the frontier informing him of his projected visit and that he had replied that every one who wanted to was free to come to Persia, and no permission was required.[170] The exchange does not give the impression that Afghani reached Tehran as the Shah's guest.

Amin al-Sultan went on to describe how Afghani had gone to stay on the outskirts of Tehran in the house of Haji Mohammed Hassan, the Master of the Mint and a follower of his, and how Afghani had written to him to say that he was the Minister's guest, that he longed to pay his respects and receive his instructions. Amin al-Sultan described Afghani as an "intriguer of the vilest type" and would have nothing to do with him. Instead, he sent for the Dragoman of the Russian Legation and enquired whether Afghani had a mission from the Russian Government. The Dragoman promised to enquire, and came back to deny such a mission:

"Since this communication from the Russian Legation, the Amin perceives a change in the language used by Sheikh Jemal, who no longer advertises himself as the agent of the Russian Government to the people of Persia".

But a little while later Morier in St. Petersburg reported that his Persian colleague complained that Afghani was doing much mischief "posing at Tehran as under the protection of Russia, and is undoubtedly trying to further Russian interests there".[171] And when a year later Afghani was deported from Persia, the Dragoman of the Russian Legation called upon Amin al-Sultan complaining that the "Syed had been arrested and banished at the instigation of the British Legation". When Amin al-Sultan enquired on what ground the Russians were protesting, since Afghani was a Persian subject, the Dragoman dropped the subject.[172]

Afghani and 'Abduh

Afghani's activities during his year in Tehran bear some analogy to his activities in Cairo during 1878-9. Persia at that particular moment, it is true, was not in the deep financial waters in which Egypt found herself towards the end of Isma'il's reign, but she was patently misgoverned, and, what is more significant, increasing European contacts made the official and literate classes less willing to acquiesce in a state of affairs which previous generations would have resigned themselves to accept. The situation was further exacerbated, in one way or another, by the direct and indirect consequences, intended or not, of Anglo-Russian rivalry, then at its height, in Central Asia. And as in Cairo, it is difficult to disentangle Afghani's motives and aims. It is clear that he worked against the Shah and Amin al-Sultan. To whose profit? To that of Amin al-Daulah's, perhaps: he had, as may be recalled, procured for Afghani an audience with the Shah; and Amin al-Daulah, we may observe, was then taking part with other notables, in a campaign of denunciation against his rival.[173] To the profit of the Russians also, as may reasonably be concluded from the Russian Dragoman's intervention when Afghani was deported; Amin al-Sultan, we may add, was at that moment in the bad books of the Russians, who denounced him as a tool of the British.[174] But again, as in Cairo, we may suspect that Afghani thought that he would be able to use those who hoped to use him, and that, in the end, power whether overt or covert, would be in his grasp. At any rate, he seems to have preached the same gospel of esoteric infidelity and political activism which he did in Cairo some twelve years before. Browne, drawing on Persian sources, describes Afghani's teaching and his entourage when, finding himself checkmated by Amin al-Sultan, he took refuge in the Shrine of Shah Abdul Azim, where he remained for seven months, a vocal opponent of the régime, until he compelled the Shah to violate the sanctity of the Shrine by having him seized and deported:

> "His hostility to the Shah", writes Browne, "was now declared: he denounced him in speech and writing, advocated his deposition, and gathered round himself a number of disciples, of whom twelve were especially prominent. Amongst these were included Shaykh Ali, one of the chief judges (*qadi-i-Adliyya*) in the time of the first National Assembly of Persia . . . ; Mirza Aqa Khan, afterwards sub-editor of the Persian *Akhtar* ('Star') at Constantinople, ultimately put to death secretly at Tabriz with Shaykh Ahmad of Kirman on

July 17, 1896; Mirza Riza of Kirman, who shot Nasiru'd-Din Shah on May 1, 1896, and was hanged at Tehran on August 12 of the same year; and Mirza Muhammad Ali Khan of Tehran, who composed a work in refutation of religions (*Radd-i-Madhahib*)."[175]

When Afghani was expelled from Persia, he came to London, probably because Malkam Khan, his lottery concession (for which a British syndicate had paid £40,000)[176]* cancelled, and himself dismissed as Ambassador, was engaged there in writing and publishing propaganda against Nasir al-Din. Afghani was soon prominent in these activities writing in English periodicals, and in Malkam Khan's Persian newspapers, and sending inflammatory letters to the Shi'ite divines to incite them, in the name of religion, against the Shah who was selling the country to the foreigner, calling upon them to depose him, since obedience to him was unlawful, and his exercise of power a danger to Islam. The divines are flattered in these letters by being described as the natural leaders of Muslims and the guarantee of the safety of Islamic states, and incited by being told that Nasir al-Din had persecuted men of religion, and that if he is deposed his successor will obey them; and to emphasise the Islamic character of these manifestos, Afghani signed himself al-Sayyid al-Husaini, underlining his alleged descent from the Prophet.[177] The Shah protested repeatedly and forcefully to the British government against Afghani being allowed to carry on such activities in London; it was, no doubt, difficult for him to credit the protestations of the Foreign Office that the law would allow them to do nothing against Afghani, and he must have thought that Afghani for some reason had the countenance of the British government, who wished to use him as a weapon against himself. Correspondence was going to and fro when Afghani solved the difficulty by leaving London for Istanbul in July, 1892.[178]

Afghani's epistles to the divines were written in Arabic, leading one to assume that they were destined for those Shi'ites who lived in the Ottoman Empire notably in Karbala and Najaf. His propaganda against the Shah in London brought him a new patron. When he went to Istanbul in the summer of 1892, it was to become a pensioner of the Sultan and to further his claim to the

* Browne mentions this concession to illustrate the financial methods of the Shah, but writes, whether in holy pretence or holy simplicity, that he does not know the identity of the Persian to whom the concession was granted.

Caliphate among the Shi'ite leaders of Mesopotamia.[179] This is the testimony of the Babi refugees in Istanbul who formed his circle and collaborated with him in propaganda against the Shah;[180]* it is likewise the testimony of the murderer of Nasir al-Din Shah who was a disciple of Afghani's from 1890, and who confessed that he committed the deed at Afghani's instigation. He told how from Istanbul Afghani entered into correspondence with the divines of Najaf and Karbala to convince them to unite under the Caliphate; how the Shah, in retaliation fomented dissension between Shi'ites and Sunnis in Samarra, how the Sultan summoned Afghani and asked him to do "whatever you can" in regard to the Shah and not to be "anxious about anything", and how thereupon Afghani incited Mirza Riza saying: "How poor-spirited you were, and how great was your love of life! You should have killed the tyrant! Why did you not kill him?"[181] These, clearly, are the outpourings of fervor and conviction. Mirza Riza revered and admired his master to the end, and went to his death in Afghani's cause. He speaks therefore with the authority of the simple-hearted; indeed it is not he who speaks, rather it is Afghani speaking through him. But, of course, the motive with which Afghani armed his disciple need not have been the only, or the most potent, one; it may well be that Afghani's exacerbated craving for power made ever more imperious by constant failure, in the end found release and fulfilment in this assassination. It remains, at any rate, Afghani's only successful political scheme.

Apart from his campaign against the Shah, Afghani seems, at one stage, to have tried to persuade the Sultan to let him carry on an agitation against British treatment of the Muslims, particularly in Egypt, but the Sultan's advisers were fearful of its consequences, and Afghani was not allowed to proceed.[182] Soon, he found himself at loggerheads with some of these advisers, notably

* Many writers, including Browne, say that Afghani was opposed to Babism, and some adduce, in proof of this, an article hostile to Babism which Afghani is supposed to have written for Butrus al-Bustani's *Encyclopaedia*. But the article, published in 1881, in Vol. V of Bustani's *Da'irat al-Ma'arif* (Beirut, 1881), well-informed and ironically sceptical, seems rather to have been written by Bustani himself. All that connects it with Afghani is the last sentence, which says: "This is what the well-known Sayyid Jamal al-Din al-Afghani and others have related concerning them." It may, of course be true that, sceptic as he was, Afghani had little use for the involved and turgid speculations of the Bab, but this would not prevent him from collaborating with his followers in a political cause.

Abu'l Huda and Shaikh As'ad. The causes of their quarrels are obscure, but it seems reasonable to assume that whatever form they took, their substance concerned power and position in the Sultan's *entourage*. His enemies seem to have succeeded, towards the end of 1895, in rousing the Sultan's suspicions against him and, as has been seen, he appealed to the British Ambassador for protection as an Afghan subject. In a letter of 19 November which he wrote to Sir Philip Currie, he attempted to make it appear as though his cause was the same as that of the Armenian Christians, for whom sympathy was then so strong in England. He said he had spent a lifetime in uprooting fanaticism, "the most serious malady of this country", and to spread the benefits of tolerance. For no reason that he could understand he was now suspect to the Sultan, and under house arrest, and it behoved Her Majesty's Ambassador to rescue him, a well-meaning, harmless, trusting, persecuted stranger.[183]* As has been seen, Sir Philip Currie was not taken in, but it is characteristic of the adroit lifetime conspirator to have swiftly and neatly outwitted him by obtaining his passport regardless. It is also characteristic of his mythomania that this devious and underhand attempt to escape from his patron should by him or his followers be represented quite otherwise. Shakib Arslan, who knew him in his last years at Istanbul, has recounted how, when the Sultan's persecution became unbearable, Afghani sent to Fitzmaurice, the Dragoman at the British Embassy, to request his help in reaching a ship leaving Istanbul:

> "Fitzmaurice came to see him and engaged himself to fulfil all Afghani's requests. The Sultan then came to hear of it, and sent him one of his chamberlains to implore him in the name of Islam not to seek foreign protection and thus impair the dignity of the Caliph. Zeal for Islam then inflamed Afghani, and having already prepared his bags for the journey, he now said to Fitzmaurice that he was giving up the idea, and let what will happen."[184]

In the event, Afghani was not able to make use of the passport, but stayed in Istanbul to encompass the death of the Shah, and himself to die, mistrusted, ineffective, querulous, in March 1897. His death was the occasion of the same calumny and intrigue which are the hallmark of his life, for his followers, whether inspired by him or not, put it about that the Sultan had murdered him. There seems to be no reason to believe in this accusation.

*See Appendix III for the text of this letter.

Afghani and 'Abduh 63

The adventures of Afghani's corpse make a worthy appendix to his history. He was presumably buried in Istanbul, and his resting place remained undisturbed until the advent of the American millionaire Charles Crane, a man of little judgment and unconsidered enthusiasms. Crane had heard of Afghani's fame and wished to make a pilgrimage to the tomb of so eminent a Muslim. He searched for the tomb in the cemeteries of Istanbul and could not find it; at last someone offered to show it to him and he was led to a plot of ground absolutely unmarked and informed that here rested Jamal al-Din[185]. On the faith of the assertion, Crane proceeded to erect on this spot a monument in memory of the Sage. Subsequently, in 1944, the Afghan government claimed the body and transported it to Kabul, where it lies. Whether what was moved from Istanbul to Kabul was Jamal al-Din's body, or whether the monument at Kabul, in seeking to do honour to someone who, in any case, was not an Afghan, was merely sheltering the remains of some unknown Muslim, God alone knows. The double misapprehension is one which would have certainly pleased Afghani.

The actual career of the Sage of the East is then seen to be quite unlike his legend. What this career portended, political activism and the transformation of religion into a political ideology, has now come to pass and its consequences are visible all around us. What is also worth noticing is that this man and his followers who, on any reckoning, must be considered subverters of Islam as the orthodox have understood and practised it, have seldom if at all had their doctrines criticised, let alone refuted, by the representatives of orthodoxy. These, on the contrary, have, with a common voice, sung Afghani's and 'Abduh's praises, and have described them as the initiators of an Islamic renaissance rescuing the faith from a secular stagnation. The best known author of such eulogies is Muhammad Rashid Rida, whose orthodoxy is considered unimpeachable, and whose attitude therefore calls for some explanation. In his *Tarikh*, Rashid Rida quotes a letter which he wrote to Afghani while he was still a young man in Qalamun; in it he says that those things which others counted against Afghani, he himself counted in his favour, and proceeding to give examples, he mentions that Afghani was reproached for being a mason, for sitting in coffee shops, for lengthy residence in Europe, and for allowing into his circle and for instructing non-Muslims in Islamic countries.[186] It would seem then that the later guardian of strict orthodoxy had in his youth some radical leanings, which made him a fervent follower of Afghani and 'Abduh. But anyone acquainted with Rashid Rida's style of writing and polemic would agree that he had a weakness for being right, and consistently right. Owing to this, a change of opinions and attitudes—and the attentive reader will detect many such in Rashid Rida's writings—is seldom conceded or explicitly registered. Again, we must remember that it was under 'Abduh's protection and patronage that he began his long and eminent career in Egypt, and that he kept his memory in ever-grateful veneration. But there is something else, perhaps more important, which may have inclined Rashid Rida, orthodox as he was, to acclaim Afghani and 'Abduh as Islamic heroes regardless of their doctrines. Islam, in contrast to Christianity and post-exilic Judaism, holds political power to be a religious value, and Muslims are loth to question the orthodoxy of those holding power, still less of those who claim to be defending Islam against hereditary enemies and to be providing weapons for its defence. Such precisely was Afghani's and 'Abduh's claim. It is highly interesting to see the manner in which Rashid Rida dealt with the allegation that 'Abduh was an agnostic and that he had favoured political assassination. Both allegations occur in Cromer's *Modern Egypt*, and Rashid Rida took them up in the course of a lengthy review of the work when it appeared in an Arabic translation; in neither case does he categorically deny, but rather in one case turns the question of faith into one of works, and in the other condones and palliates. It is well-known, argues Rashid Rida, that 'Abduh devoted his life to the service of Egypt and Islam and that he believed himself to be the instrument whereby Islam would return to its pristine glory: how then can we doubt his faith or accuse him of agnosticism or atheism?[187] Even more curious than this worldly and utilitarian apology is Rashid Rida's view of political assassination. It is entirely characteristic that he should, in the first place, criticise Blunt—who had published 'Abduh's report of his talk with Afghani in 1879 on the possibility of killing the Khedive Isma'il—for divulging a private confidence. In the second place let us, says Rashid Rida, ask an ignorant fellah, together with Aristotle, the most famous of the ancient philosophers and Herbert Spencer, the best-known among the modern, for their opinion: all three would concur that there was nothing strange or blameworthy in Afghani and his youthful disciple desiring to do away with a tyrant who was an obstacle to reform![188]

Afghani and 'Abduh

If such could be the views of Rashid Rida, then we may not be surprised by the remarkable dearth in modern Islam of that systematic, determined and informed criticism of secularist claims and assumptions which Catholic and Jewish divines opposed to the attacks of the "Enlightened".[189] The contrary has rather happened in Islam where the "Enlightened" modernists have been welcomed into the citadel of orthodoxy and hailed as its most resourceful defenders. The last word on all this may appropriately be left to Wilfrid Scawen Blunt, Afghani's and 'Abduh's friend, the champion in England of Islam and Arabism. In 1897 he went on a journey to the Sanussi oases in the Western Desert, and there apparently came to realise what Islam was like when it was practised by people who studied their eternal salvation, rather than by those who, like his friends, sought to use it as a weapon in a campaign against the British Empire.

"My experience of the Senussia at Siwah", he wrote in his diary in March, 1897, "has convinced me that there is *no* hope anywhere to be found in Islam. I had made myself a romance about these reformers, but I see that it has no substantial basis, and I shall never go further now than I am in the Mohammedan direction. The less religion in the world, perhaps, after all, the better."

And a year later, more sweepingly and more trenchantly: "The Moslems of today who believe are mere wild beasts like the men of Siwah, the rest have lost their faith."[190] Since his day, of course, a large proportion of the wild beasts, thanks no doubt to the modernists, has been civilised and domesticated. The few survivors are firmly confined to their reservations.

Appendix I

Below are found extracts from a letter which 'Abduh wrote to Afghani following his exile to Beirut, which Rashid Rida prints on pp. 599–603 of his *Tarikh*, Vol. II, 2nd ed. What Rashid Rida has printed is presumably the text of a draft found among 'Abduh's papers. The original letter itself as received by Afghani has been recently printed by Afshar and Mahdavi in *Documents*, plates 134–137: the letter as here printed shows additions to and variations from the draft printed by Rashid Rida. Also, in this version the letter enables us to fill in names suppressed by Rashid Rida in his text out of discretion. In the translation which follows, as in the study itself, I have used the text of the *Documents* in preference to that of the *Tarikh*. Those parts of the letter dealing with Egyptian politics, have been discussed and quoted in the body of the study, and the extracts which follow deal only with 'Abduh's attitude to Afghani; they constitute the opening paragraphs of the letter and its penultimate one:

"[My Exalted Lord, whom God preserve and second in his purpose!]* Would that I knew what to write to you. You know what is in my soul, as you† know what is in yours. You have made us with your hands, invested our matter with its perfect form [and created us in the best shape]‡. Through you have we known ourselves, through you have we known you, through you have we known the whole universe. Your knowledge of us is, as will not be hidden from you, a necessary knowledge, it is the knowledge you have of yourself, your confidence in your power and will; from you have we issued and to you, to you do we return.

"I have been endowed by you with a wisdom which enables me to change inclinations, impart rationality to reason, overcome great obstacles, and control the innermost thoughts of men. I have been given by you a will so powerful as to move the immovable, deal blows to the greatest of obstacles, and remain firm in the right (*haqq*) until truth (*haqq*) is satisfied. I used to imagine that my power [through your power]§ was limitless and my capacity infinite, but lo, the days have brought me endless

---

* Omitted in Rashid Rida's text.
† Rashid Rida has "I" instead.
‡ Rashid Rida may have purposely omitted this sentence since his text has three dots here.
§ Omitted in Rashid Rida's text.

Appendix I 67

surprises. I have taken up the pen to show you that in my soul with which you are more than myself familiar, but I have found myself defeated, with a paralysed heart, a trembling hand, quaking limbs and distracted thoughts, [your] mind mastering me as though, O my lord (*maulayy*), you have given me a kind of power which, to indicate the potency of your dominion (*sultan*), you have made to extend over individuals,* but excepted from its sway that which relates to communication with you, and the approach to your majestic abode (*ila maqamika al-jalil*). So far as I am concerned, you have three souls, were one of which to descend into a petrified humanity, it would transform it into the perfect man. Your visible likeness which is manifest in my imaginative faculty and which holds sway over my combined senses [is one]—it is the picture of nobility, the image of wisdom, and the temple of perfection—; to it refer all my *sensibilia*, and in it are lost (*funiyat*) all my visual impressions. [Another one of your souls is] the spirit of your wisdom with which you have resuscitated what was dead in us, illumined our minds, and graced our spirits, nay, the spirit through which you have dwelt in us and been made manifest through our persons, so that we were your numerals and you were the One, we the absence and you the witness. [The third soul is] your photograph which [in the shrine of my prayers (*fi qiblat salati*)]† I set up as a censor over all my actions, to exercise sway over me in all my circumstances;‡ I never did an action or spoke a word, never aimed at some objective or abandoned it, until your souls—which are three—concurred in the decision. I have, then, followed the direction of these souls in striving for the good, in exalting the word of truth (*haqq*), and in supporting the power of wisdom and the rule of virtue. In all this I was nothing but an instrument to execute this triple command; I in myself had no independent will, and this triple command could not therefore become quadrupled. The high powers [of your inspiration] have forsaken me§ in my

---

* Rashid Rida notes that at this point the text is uncertain.

† Omitted in Rashid Rida's text.

‡ Rashid Rida notes here that this photograph was confiscated by the police when 'Abduh was accused of rebellion, but that 'Abduh subsequently obtained another which he used to keep in his study "in memory of that noble spirit who imparted to him this new and superior education which made him strive all through his life for the cause of God the Most High".

§ *takhallat 'anni*. Rashid Rida has *tamaththalat 'anni*, which is clearly an inferior reading.

correspondence with you, and have interposed themselves between me and my soul, in fulfilment of the law that the effect does not have any influence over its own cause. At any rate, the letters received by the lord from his slave are nothing but a kind of prayer and supplication; I do not suppose that they contain anything to clarify a mystery, or contribute to greater understanding. My intercessor for any weakness of expression here is nothing stronger than that the mind is too feeble to fix its gaze upon you, and thought too timid to stand without fear before you; but what intercessor is stronger than your mercy towards the weak, and your compassion for shame and modesty?"

"[As far as concerns us, I understand the situation of my lord. Even though his eloquence is powerful enough to make angels doubt the object of their adoration and prophets their inspiration, yet it is not in his power himself to throw doubt on himself, or to convince his high reason of impossibilities, even though it was in his power to persuade any one he desired, whether Eastern or Western, of such impossibility.]*

"The judgement of my lord concerning the faithlessness of the Egyptians is confirmed by evidences and witnessed by events, but we are not like them; for you have taken us out of our nature, and changed us into a strange plant (*nabtan ghariban*) which is not nourished in that earth and does not grow in its atmosphere; which rather flourishes where fate allows it some like elements to strengthen its constitution, and enable it to flower and produce goodly fruit. Otherwise it wilts and dies, or else is uprooted and exiled out of the country."†

The letter ends with a request for Afghani's photograph, copies of his articles, and letters "from your noble pen"; "They

---

* This passage does not appear in Rashid Rida's text.

† The whole of this paragraph is possibly very significant. The terms *nawabit* (plants self-grown in alien soil) and *ghuraba'* (strangers) are found in Muslim philosophical and mystical writings to denote those who have attained true wisdom, and hence are exiles in this gross and degenerating world. The terms *gharib*, *ghuraba'*, are traced to the sufis, while *nabit* and *nawabit* are derived, as E. I. J. Rosenthal argues, from Plato, *Republic*, 520, where Plato describes the condition of the philosophers in unjust states: "For there they are spontaneous growths, and their city's constitution has only hampered them, and it seems fair that the self-sown plant which is debtor to no man for its culture should not be eager to pay the price of its culture to anybody." See E. I. J. Rosenthal, *Political Thought in Medieval Islam*, Cambridge, 1958, pp. 318 and 172.

Appendix 1

will be kept as we keep your secret, and deposited where we have deposited your affection." The text of the *Documents* discloses that 'Abduh had two copies of Afghani's photograph, one of which was, as has been seen, confiscated by the police; the other he had lent to another disciple, Sa'd Zaghlul, who had begged for it, "and, taking pity on him, I let him have it for a matter of days in order that it might enable him to live for years". The articles which 'Abduh requests may have been those which Rashid Rida reproduced in *al-Manar*, Vol. XXV (1924), pp. 756–760, stating that his source was a manuscript copy [made by 'Abduh?] and that they had appeared in *al-Nahla*, no. 3, Vol. V. According to Rashid Rida, Afghani wrote these articles during his stay in London at the end of 1882 and the beginning of 1883. One of the two articles, *asbab al-harb fi misr* ("The Causes of the War in Egypt") Rashid Rida stated to have been unsigned, but that authorship was ascribed to Afghani by the copyist; whether the other article, *al-siyasa al-ingiliziyya fi'l-mamalik al-sharqiyya* ("English Policy in Oriental Kingdoms") was signed Rashid Rida does not say. I have been unable to see the no. of *al-Nahla* where these articles are said to have appeared; the British Museum holding of this periodical runs from 1877 to 1880 only.

Appendix II

1.

Lettre sur L'Hindoustan (L'INSTRANSIGEANT, *24 April, 1883*)

Au mois d'août dernier *l'Intransigeant*, le premier, a fait connaître au public parisien le cheik afghan Djamal-ed-Dine, dont notre collaborateur E. Vauquelin, dans ses *Souvenirs de la Révolution d'Egypte*, terminait ainsi le portrait:

"Un soir, dans la mosquée Hassan, au Caire, devant quatre mille personnes, il prononça un discours véhément dans lequel il dénonçait, avec un sens prophétique profond, trois ans à l'avance, le but final de la politique anglaise sur les bords du Nil.

"Il montrait en même temps le khédive Thewfik Pacha comme le serviteur conscient ou inconscient mais forcé des ambitions anglaises, et il terminait par un cri de guerre contre l'étranger et un appel à la révolution pour sauver l'indépendence de l'Egypte et fonder sa liberté.

"Sur la demande du consul général d'Angleterre, deux jours après l'orateur de la mosquée Hassan était arrêté conduit à bord d'un navire et transporté a Djeddah sur la côte d'Arabie.

"Djamal-ed-Din se retira dans l'intérieur de la province du Hedjaz, et l'on n'entendit plus parler de lui.

"Si Djamal-ed-Dine n'est pas mort en soldat d'aventures sur quelque champ de bataille inconnu de l'Asie, ou s'il n'a pas été empoisonné, il reparaîtra bientôt, et l'Angleterre contre lequel il a fait le serment d'Annibal, le reconnaîtra sans peine aux coups qu'il lui portera. Sur quel point?—sur l'Indus, peut-être."

Il y a quelques semaines, nous avons annoncé l'arrivée à Paris du cheik afghan, qui nous a promis sur la situation dans l'Hindoustan, où il a vécu plusieurs années et qu'il vient de parcourir récemment encore, des notes et des renseignements dont on pourra apprécier le vif intérêt.

Voici la première lettre que nous adresse notre *correspondant occasionnel*, comme disent les Anglais.

Le but principal des Anglais dans ces dernières années a été de se rendre maîtres de tous les chemins qui conduisent aux Indes.

C'est pour cela qu'ils ont tenté de s'emparer naguère des défilés de l'Afghanistan et du Belouchistan, c'est pour cela que maintenant ils essaient de s'établir en Egypte.

L'explication de la politique suivie à cet égard en Orient par la Grande-Bretagne est dans la vive inquiétude que ressent cette

Appendix II

puissance pour le maintien de sa domination sur l'Hindoustan et dans la crainte qu'elle éprouve de se voir déposséder dans un avenir plus ou moins prochain de son magnifique domaine indien.

C'est cette préoccupation, dominant toutes les autres, qui pousse les Anglais dans une voie où ils froissent continuellement d'autres nations et qui les conduit à prendre une attitude bien faite pour éveiller la surprise et les légitimes susceptibilités de tous les hommes d'Etat qui ne sont pas anglais.

On sait, en effet, en Angleterre que tous les habitants des Indes sans distinction de race, de caste ou de religion; les musulmans aussi bien que les sectateurs de Brahma ou de Boudha; les princes comme les portefaix, ont tous au même degré la haine des oppressurs étrangers, et ceux-ci sont bien convaincus qu'un seul coup de canon, qu'un seul coup de fusil tiré sur un point quelconque de la côte ou de la frontière de l'Hindoustan suffirait pour faire éclater un soulèvement général, depuis Ceylan jusqu'aux pieds de l'Himalaya, et à déterminer instantanément tous les Hindous à faire cause commune avec le peuple, quel qu'il soit, qui attaquera les Anglais dans l'Inde.

Ces derniers ignorent si peu à quel point leur domination est fragile; ils connaissent si bien et les dispositions hostiles de leurs sujets hindous et la faiblesse numérique de leurs forces militaires dans l'Inde et ailleurs, qu'ils voudraient isoler moralement l'Hindoustan du reste du monde en entourant cette contrée d'une sorte de muraille, par toutes les entraves qu'ils apportent à la circulation des voyageurs à quelque nationalité qu'ils appartiennent, craignant sans doute que les étrangers ne découvrent et ne révèlent le secret de la faiblesse des Anglais cachée sous une puissance apparente.

Constamment préoccupés de maintenir leur domination chancelante, les maîtres de l'Inde n'ont cependant jamais cherché là où ils auraient pu les trouver, les moyens de consolider leur domination.

Bien loin de travailler à gagner les sympathies des peuples, ils n'ont jamais cessé de les froisser de toutes les manières dans leurs intérêts.

Les Anglais règnent sur les Indes depuis plus de cent ans et, depuis ce temps-là, les Hindous sont mis pour ainsi dire hors l'humanité, ne pouvant aspirer à aucun grade militaire, à aucune fonction politique, n'ayant pas même la liberté la plus sacrée de toutes: la liberté de conscience.

Au lieu d'alléger les impôts de façon que les malheureux

Hindous ne travaillent pas uniquement pour le fisc, et puissent au moins conserver de leurs faibles gains de quoi subvenir à leurs besoins, les Anglais ont anéanti le commerce et l'industrie des indigènes par les importations de leurs fabriques d'Europe, et rompu les relations entre l'Inde et l'Afghanistan, son voisin en déclarant aux Afghans une guerre injuste et déloyale dans laquelle, du reste, ils ont complètement échoué.

La conséquence de cette guerre impolitique, c'est que maintenant les Afghans sont devenus les ennemis implacables des Anglais, contre lesquels ils ont fait alliance avec la Russie pour agir avec celle-ci quand sonnera l'heure favorable.

N'ayant pas réussi en Afghanistan et voyant d'autre part d'un oeil jaloux les Français occuper la Tunisie; sentant grandir tous les jours chez les Hindous une haine capable dès à présent de jeter ceux-ci dans les bras de la première puissance qui voudra attaquer l'Angleterre au coeur de ses possessions asiatiques, les Anglais, aveuglés sans doute par les dangers qui menacent leur impuissance, viennent de commettre une faute dont la double conséquence sera pour eux désastreuse dans l'avenir.

Cette faute, c'est leur intervention récente sur la terre des Pharaons par la ruse et la fourberie—les seules armes redoutables de l'Angleterre—avec l'arrière-pensée d'étendre leur prépondérance de l'autre côté de la mer Rouge sur les provinces de l'Hedjaz et de l'Yemen, en Arabie, où ils possèdent déjà Aden.

La première conséquence de l'intervention anglaise en Egypte a été de blesser plusieurs nations européennes et spécialement la France, dont les intérêts sont incontestablement considérables dans la vallée du Nil.

Les Anglais n'auraient pas dû oublier, cependant, quelle que soit l'idée qu'ils aient de leur puissance, que l'amitié du peuple français est indispensable en prévision des événement dont l'Orient peut être prochainement le théâtre, tandis que la France peut très facilement se passer de l'amitié de la nation anglaise. La perte des sympathies françaises, c'est assurément une des plus grandes erreurs commises par cet homme d'Etat à courte vue qui s'appelle M. Gladstone.

Le second résultat, également funeste pour l'Angleterre, de son intervention en Egypte, c'est l'impression d'indignation et de colère que cet acte brutal a produite dans tout le monde musulman, et particulièrement chez les musulmans des Indes.

La vénération de ceux-ci pour le sultan actuel, et en général pour le Kalife régnant, quel qu'il soit, est un sentiment qui leur

Appendix II

est commun avec tous les croyants de l'Islam. Cette vénération est en quelque sort un dogme de la religion mahométane et dans toutes les mosquées, chaque vendredi, à la prière, les musulmans commencent par invoquer Allah pour la conservation des jours du Sultan-Kalife.

Les Anglais n'ont certainement pas oublié qu'à l'époque où ils sont entrés en Egypte, un commencement d'insurrection a eu lieu à Mirit et que le mouvement aurait rapidement gagné l'Inde musulmane entière, s'ils n'avaient eu l'adresse de calmer les esprits en répandant à profusion des manifestes où ils déclaraient combattre Arabi, seulement parce qu'il était rebelle, et entrer en Egypte uniquement pour obéir aux ordres du Sultan.

Cette comédie a réussi, il est vrai.

Mais elle n'aurait plus le même succès si on voulait la reprendre; surtout si les Turcs, ouvrant les yeux, avaient acquis le certitude que l'Angleterre veut s'annexer l'Egypte, c'est-à-dire la partie la plus importante de leur empire en Afrique, pour enlever ensuite Hedjaz et l'Yemen à l'autorité musulmane et placer ces provinces sous la domination britannique.

Certains de la sympathie de leurs coreligionnaires des Indes, les Ottomans ne manqueront pas, dans ce cas, de soutenir la politique de la grande puissance dont les vues ambitieuses sont tournées sans cesse vers les Indes, même s'ils ne devaient pas gagner à cette politique autre chose que la satisfaction de faire échec à une nation qui travaille au démembrement de leur empire.

Dans le monde gouvernemental, on sait très bien en Angleterre que le sultan poussé à bout serait un allié précieux pour les adversaires des Anglais dans les Indes, rien qu'en faisant prêcher à la Mecque et en envoyant dans l'Hindoustan un manifeste porté par quelque cheik autorisé à parler en son nom.

Mais, même en laissant de côté ces combinaisons éventuelles de la diplomatie de Stamboul, le seul fait de l'occupation de l'Egypte, qui est le chemin de la Mecque, et le désir secret mais certain qu'ont les Anglais d'étendre leur domination sur la contrée de l'Hedjaz et de l'Yemen, à la fois berceau et citadelle de l'Islamisme, suffiraient pour décider les musulmans indiens à faire dès maintenant cause commune avec n'importe quelle puissance qui envahira l'Inde anglaise.

Et que les Anglais ne se fassent pas l'illusion de croire qu'ils pourraient, dans cette conjoncture, opposer aux musulmans des Indes leurs compatriotes appartenant aux autres cultes. Ils se tromperaient étrangement.

Courbés depuis tant d'années sous le même joug, abreuvés des humiliations, plongés par l'insatiable rapacité du conquérant dans une commune misère tous les Hindous, vienne le jour des revendications, seront unis dans l'action, comme ils sont aujourd'hui unis dans la haine.

A l'appui de ce que je viens de dire, combien d'examples et de preuves ne trouverais-je pas dans le passé et, sans chercher davantage, est-ce que dans la grande révolte de 1857, Nana-Sahib, qui n'était pas musulman, ne s'est pas montré un ennemi plus acharné des Anglais que n'étaient Firouz-Shah et la Begum Saheh?

Cette solidarité, cette union que j'affirme peut sembler douteuse à ceux qui ignorent les moyens qu'emploient les Anglais pour gouverner, administrer et exploiter les Indes.

Afin de répondre sur ce point, je ferai connaitre dans un prochain article des faits et des détails dont la précision ne laissera je l'espère de doute dans l'esprit de personne.

Cheik-Djamal-Eddin

2.

Le Mahdi (L'INTRANSIGEANT, *8 December, 1883*)

L'année dernière, *l'Intransigeant* a, le premier, fait connaître au public parisien l'une des personnalités les plus remarquables et l'une des plus hautes intelligences du monde oriental, le cheik afghan Gemal-ed-Din, le redoutable adversaire que l'Angleterre rencontre partout, et qui semble avoir fait contre elle le serment d'Annibal. On se rappelle ce fait, cité par notre collaborateur E. Vauquelin, dans ses *Souvenirs de la Révolution d'Egypte:* Un soir dans la mosquée Hassan, au Caire, devant quatre mille personnes, Gemal-ed-Din prononça un discours véhément dans lequel il dénonçait, avec un sens prophétique profond, trois ans à l'avance, le but final de la politique anglaise sur les bords du Nil. Sur la demande du consul général d'Angleterre, deux jours après, l'orateur de la mosquée Hassan était arrêté, conduit à bord d'un navire et transporté à Djeddah, sur la côte d'Arabie. Gemal-ed-Din se retira dans l'intérieur de la province du Hedjaz et l'on n'entendit plus parler de lui.

Il y a quelques mois, le cheik afghan arrivait à Paris, et il nous donnait, sur la situation dans l'Hindoustan, où il a vécu plusieurs années et qu'il venait de parcourir récemment encore, des notes et des renseignements dont on a pu apprécier le vif

Appendix II

intérêt. Aujourd'hui, il veut bien nous communiquer une étude sur le Mahdi dont l'apparition sur le Nil-Blanc a révolutionné l'Islam, et qui vient d'infliger à l'armée anglo-égyptienne la plus sanglante défaite. Cette étude, nous la publions telle qu'elle nous a été remise, sans y rien ajouter, sans en rien retrancher. Nul mieux que le célèbre cheik afghan n'était capable de l'écrire, car personne ne connaît mieux que lui le monde musulman et n'est plus à même de prévoir les graves conséquences que les événements du Soudan peuvent avoir en Egypte, et ailleurs aussi.

I

L'homme obscur, *Mohamed Ahmed*, qui, sous le nom de Mahdi, a paru il y a deux ans dans le Soudan, vient, par l'anéantissement presque complet de la dernière expédition, commandée par le général Hicks de préoccuper l'opinion générale de l'Europe et d'alarmer particulièrement la presse anglaise qui reflète, dans l'état actuel des choses, les véritables sentiments de la nation.

Cette victoire, qui a jeté le trouble dans le Foreign-Office, semble réserver à M. Gladstone, dans la vallée du Nil, les mêmes fruits qu'a obtenus lord Beaconsfield en Afghanistan. Elle a, en outre, ouvert la porte aux convoitises de l'ex-khédive Ismail ainsi que de Halim-Pacha. Chacun d'eux travaille activement à entrer dans les bonnes grâces de l'Angleterre, lui promettant d'être à même d'étouffer cette insurrection, à condition qu'elle lui assure son appui pour arriver au khédiviat.

Quant à Towfik, il se trouve dans une situation extrêmement compliquée et dans un état qui devient, de jour en jour, plus critique. On voit ce malheureux prince sous le coup de deux éventualités également funestes: l'occupation définitive de l'Egypte par les Anglais, ou bien l'arrivée du Mahdi au Caire; et entre deux ambitions: celle de son père Ismail et celle de son grand-oncle Halim.

Je me propose d'émettre, dans un prochain article, certaines appréciations personnelles sur le Mahdi au point de vue politique, au point de vue des intérêts des puissances coloniales et de la Turquie, et de parler de l'impression que pourrait produire son nom dans le monde musulman, ainsi que des intentions de l'Angleterre dans cette grave question et du profit que croient pouvoir réaliser les personnes qui ambitionnent le khédiviat. Mais je me bornerai, pour le moment, à esquisser certains faits historiques qui sont de nature à intéresser le public et à l'édifier sur le Mahdi, sa puissance sur les musulmans, leur manière d'y croire, les causes qui ont amené ces croyances, les événements de même nature qui se sont produits dans le passé, et enfin sur ce que l'Islam attend actuellement du Mahdi.

Le Mahdi—mot arabe signifiant: inspiré par Dieu pour suivre le vrai chemin—n'est pas un prophète, comme le prétendent certains journaux; il n'est considéré chez les musulmans que comme un des descendants du grand Prophète, pieux, dévot, suivant la ligne qu'a tracée son aieul Mohamed respectant la doctrine musulmane. Sa mission divine serait de supprimer les *Bidahs*—innovations dans la religion—de proclamer la justice, d'établir l'égalité entre tous les croyants et de propager le nom de l'Islam, en le mettant en relief dans toutes les parties du monde. On le nomme aussi en arabe *Kaim-Al-Mohamed*, ce qui veut dire:—celui qui, des descendants du grand Prophète, se lève pour soutenir la foi musulmane.

La croyance en la venue d'un Mahdi est répandue dans toutes les contrées mahométanes sans aucune distinction de secte. Elle est d'autant plus enracinée chez les peuples islamites qu'elle se maintient depuis le premier siècle de l'hégire.

El-Feberi[191] et Ibn-El-Essir, deux des plus célèbres historiens musulmans et des plus respectés, ont publié dans leurs écrits que les croyants, vers le milieu du premier siècle de l'Hégire, disaient de Omar, fils d'Abdul-Aziz, parent du Prophète et l'un des plus justes des khalifats de Beni-Omaia, que, si ce n'est lui le Mahdi attendu, ce ne pourrait être que Jésus, fils de Marie, qui reparaîtrait avant la fin du monde.

L'attente de la venue d'un Mahdi s'accentue tellement chez les musulmans, toutes les fois qu'ils se trouvent dans une gêne et qu'ils se voient menacés dans leur religion ou dominés par une puissance étrangère, qu'ils ressemblent alors à un homme égaré, par une nuit obscure, dans un vaste désert, attendant avec impatience l'apparition d'une étoile qui le guide.

D'ailleurs, ces croyances sont basées sur des versets de traditions innombrables et très respectées, attribués au grand prophète Mohamed. Ces versets ont été cités dans plus d'un livre, entre autres: *El-Mousned*, de l'Imam Ahmed Ibn-Hambal, le Sunniste, l'un des fondateurs des quatre sectes musulmanes, *El-Sahih* du Seid Aly El-Tormozi, *Mousned Firdans*[192] et *Ibn-Maja*, etc., etc.

Tous les savants musulmans, sauf Ibn-Khaldoun dans sa préface et quelques autres dont le nombre est fort limité, ont été unanimes à reconnaître l'authenticité de ces traditions. Il ressort de ces livres que le grand prophète Mohamed a parlé du Mahdi

Appendix II

en maints endroits, l'appelant tantôt *El-Mahdi*, et tantôt *El-Kaim*. Il a dit: "S'il ne restait pour la fin du monde qu'un seul jour, ce jour sera prolongé par Dieu jusqu'à l'apparition d'un de mes parents, dont la mission serait de raffermir ma religion et de propager ma foi." Dans un autre verset, il a dit: "Le Kaim (el Mahdi) sera un de mes descendants et vous prodiguera sans mesure toutes sortes de biens." Et dans un autre: "Il (le Mahdi) vous donnera les trésors de Rome, et la terre lui fournira ses immenses richesses." Dans un suivant: "Si l'injustice et l'iniquité se répandent dans le monde, et que le fidèle (le musulman) devienne pire qu'un esclave, attendez-vous à voir apparaître un de mes descendants, le Mahdi." Il dit encore: "Le Mahdi, un de mes parents, apparaîtra dans les moments difficiles et comblera le monde d'équité et de justice après avoir été rempli d'injustice et d'iniquité." Ailleurs, il est dit: "Si Benou-El-Asfar (les fils du jaune—le prophète faisait allusion aux anciens Romains) vous dominent, attendez El-Kaim de ma famille." Voici encore un autre verset: "Le Mahdi est de nous, son nom sera le mien (Mahomed) le nom de son Père sera le nom du mien (Abdullah), et le nom de sa mère sera le nom de la mienne, (Amina)".

Plusieurs autres versets du même genre démontrent d'une manière non moins évidente la certitude de la venue d'un Mahdi.

Quant aux citations qui ont été faites par plusieurs saints et dévots prétendant en avoir reçu l'inspiration divine, lesquelles démontrent que le Mahdi ou El-Kaim apparaîtra de l'est ou de l'ouest, de la Mecque ou du Koufa, et fixent à telle ou telle autre époque son apparition, elles sont tellement multiples et diverses que je n'ai pas jugé à propos de les relater.

Il a paru, sous le nom du Mahdi ou de El-Kaim, plus d'une centaine d'individus, dans tous les siècles et dans tous les pays musulmans. Et bien que la plupart d'entre eux n'aient pas réussi, il s'en est trouvé, cependant, qui on formé des royaumes que leurs descendants ont maintenus pendant plusieurs siècles:

Abou-Muslem-El-Koraçani, qui a anéanti le Khalafah de Beni-Oumaia et établi le Khalafah de Beni-Abbas, n'a réussi à grouper les masses et à recruter une armée redoutable, à Merv et dans les autres pays de Khorassan, qu'en se servant du nom de Kaim-Al-Mohamed (Mahdi). Il a pu par ce moyen les engager à proclamer Abou El-Abbas El-Saffah Kalifah, lequel est le premier Kélifah de Bani El Abbas et l'un des petits-fils de Abbas, oncle du grand prophète Mohamed.

Idriss le Grand, un des patits-fils de Mahomed, qui a établi le royaume des Adaressa, au temps de Haroun El-Raschid, et a élevé la ville de Fas, n'a pu réussir aussi que sous le nom de *Kaim* al-Mohamed—C'est en cette qualité de mahdi que Obeid-Allah, aieul des Kholafahs (les souverains) fatimistes, qui a conquis le Caire, la Syrie, le Hedjaz et l'Iemen, a pu fonder ces vastes royaumes et bâtir le ville de Mahdia, qui porte encore son nom de nos jours.

Mohamed, le chef des Mouahédins—(ceux qui croient en Dieu seul)—n'a pu gagner à sa cause les Morabitouns et étendre ses conquêtes jusqu'à l'Andalousie, laissant un vaste royaume à ses successeurs, que par sa prétention d'être un *Mahdi*.

En un mot, sous ce nom, combien de personnes de l'Islam n'ont-elles pas accompli des actions éclatantes et considérables, et n'ont-elles pas amené un changement très sérieux dans le monde des croyants!

Malgré tous les mahdis qui se sont succédé jusqu'à nos jours, les musulmans en attendent toujours un nouveau.

Les chiistes Isna-Achariins, qui croient en douze Imams descendant successivement de Mohamed, comme les Persans, par exemple, tout en tombant d'accord avec les sunnistes sur la certitude de la venue d'un mahdi, diffèrent de ceux-ci sur sa personnalité. Ils disent que Mohamed El-Mahdi est le fils de Hassan-El-Ascari; le neuvième des descendants du grand Prophète, et prétendent que ce Mohamed El-Mahdi est né à Samirra (ville près de Bagdad), sous le règne du khalife El-Mutawakel El-Abbassi. Un jour, craignant les mauvaises dispositions du khalife à son égard, il se décida, à l'âge de cinq ans, à se cacher dans un puits, et pendant soixante-dix ans il correspondit avec ses partisans. Cette disparition s'appelle chez les chiistes: El-Gaibat El-Sogra, ce qui signifie: la petite disparition. Les Chiites prétendent aussi qu'à partir de cette date il rompit ses relations avec ses adeptes et ceux-ci le considèrent comme vivant jusqu'a nos jours, estimant la durée de son existence à plus de mille ans. Suivant leur doctrine, ce mahdi apparaîtra entre le Keck et El-Mokam, à la Mecque, et aura pour résidence El-Koufa (près de Bagdad), étendant la domination musulmane de l'Orient jusqu'à l'Occident.

Bref, quelques diverses que puissent être ces croyances au point de vue de la forme, il n'en est pas moins vrai que chaque musulman attend un mahdi, prêt à le suivre et à lui sacrifier sa vie, avec tout ce qu'il possède. Les musulmans indiens surtout,

Appendix II 79

étant donné les souffrances infinies et les peines cruelles qu'ils endurent sous la domination anglaise, sont ceux qui l'attendent avec le plus d'impatience.

Enfin, le prestige du Mahdi, aux yeux des musulmans, dépendra uniquement du succès final qu'il pourra obtenir.

C'est d'ailleurs le cas de tous ses devanciers.

Le cheik Gemal-Ed-Din-El-Afghan

3.

Le Mahdi (L'INTRANSIGEANT, *11 December, 1883*)

En publiant la suite de l'importante étude que le cheich Gemal-Ed-Din veut bien nous donner sur le Mahdi et les conséquences probables de son apparition victorieuse dans le Soudan, nous croyons devoir rappeler ce que nous disions il y a trois jours : cette étude est publiée telle qu'elle nous a été remise, sans que rien y ait été changé ; c'est un musulman qui l'a écrite, on ne doit pas l'oublier, et ce musulman parle en fils croyant de l'Islam. Nous avons pensé qu'il fallait conserver à ce travail son caractère particulier, et nous avons laissé parler librement l'auteur.

II

La défaite que Mohamed-Ahmed, avec ses troupes irrégulières, vient de faire subir au général Hicks, a eu pour résultat de dissiper les doutes que concevaient, à l'égard de sa personnalité, les populations de certaines contrées du Soudan. La victoire d'El-Obeid a relevé son prestige, à leurs yeux, à un tel point qu'elles considèrent comme un miracle ce qu'il vient d'accomplir.

Cet événement a, en outre, fait naître chez les Egyptiens l'espoir de se débarrasser de la domination anglaise avec l'aide du Mahdi ; de leur côté, les cheichs de l'Université d'El Azhar ont commencé à se repentir d'avoir rendu le *Fatwa* qui traitait d'imposteur Mohamed-Ahmed.

La victoire d'El-Obeid, qui a eu un immense retentissement dans le monde de l'Islam, a réveillé les sentiments religieux de tous les cheichs d'El-Tarika (confréries religieuses), comme les Kadirïa, Nakchïa, Jalalïa, Senoucïa, Chadilïa, etc., etc., lesquels exercent une grande autorité sur leurs nombreux adeptes. Ces cheichs n'attendent qu'une autre action éclatante, qui achève de les édifier sur le compte du Mahdi, pour se révolter et faire cause commune avec lui.

D'ailleurs, les soldats égyptiens étant muslmans et, par conséquent, croyant à la certitude de la venue d'un Mahdi, persuadés d'ailleurs qu'en résistant à Mohamed-Ahmed, ils ne serviraient ni leurs intérêts, ni ceux de leur pays, car seule l'Angleterre profiterait évidemment de l'échec qu'ils pourraient lui infliger, ne voudront, en aucun cas, combattre aucun des détachements du Mahdi.

Avant l'accomplissement d'une autre action éclatante—nouveau miracle qui n'a rien d'improbable, étant donné la victoire que le Mahdi a remportée sur dix mille soldats réguliers, et les proclamations qu'il a eu l'ingénieuse idée de lancer aux cheichs du Caire, de la Mecque et de la Médine—et avant l'extension des dispositions insurrectionelles religieuses, tant en Orient qu'en Occident, les Turcs seuls, à mon avis, peuvent, au nom du Khalifat, se rendre maître de la situation et prévenir des troubles graves. Mais les puissances européennes qui suivent une politique dont le résultat est obscur, ainsi que l'Angleterre, dont les intentions ne sont un secret pour personne, s'opposent énergiquement à toute intervention turque.

Si donc Mohamed Ahmed—le Mahdi—venait à remporter une autre victoire, s'il occupait Khartoum, ou encore s'il s'approchait des confins de la Haute-Egypte, il en résulterait un soulèvement général de toutes les populations arabes qui sont sous la domination ottomane; et il serait alors extrêmement difficile à la Turquie, vu sa faiblesse actuelle, d'apaiser ce soulèvement.

D'autres mouvements se produiraient sans doute sur différents points du territoire placé sous la domination turque. Je citerai notamment, parmi les groupes musulmans prêts à se soulever: le cheich El-Senouci avec ses adeptes, très nombreux à Tripoli et parmi les Arabes nomades du littoral du Hedjaz;—les Beni-Harb, tribu considérable habitant entre la Mecque et Médine;—El-Acir, entre le Hedjaz et l'Iemen;—les Zaidia, à Sanhah et à Kawkaban: —le Dahi des Ismalistes, à Nejran, dans l'Iemen;—Mohamed-About Ràchid, à Nejd, et les tribus de Aneza et Chamarr, sur les confins de Bagdad, du Moucel et de la Syrie. Toutes ces tribes, qui se soulèvent à chaque instant contre la Turquie, dont elles ne sont pas satisfaites, ne demanderont pas mieux que de profiter de l'occasion que leur fournit le Mahdi pour se débarrasser du Khalife (le sultan).

Il serait alors impossible aux Ottomans, en invoquant le nom du Khalife—seul moyen qu'ils aient à leur disposition pour maintenir sous leur domination les diverses populations musulmanes—il serait, dis-je impossible aux Ottomans d'étouffer une

Appendix II

insurrection dont les conséquences ne seraient pas à dédaigner. Les musulmans croient, en effet, que le Khalifat, qu'il soit légitime, c'est-à-dire entre les mains d'un Koraichi—un membre de la tribu de Mohamed—ou bien illégitime, c'est-à-dire entre les mains d'un conquérant, doit disparaître devant l'apparition du Mahdi, qui serait, lui, le véritable Khalife des Croyants.

Les cheichs des confréries religieuses El-Kadiria et El-Chadilia ne manqueront pas non plus, en cette occasion, d'organiser une active propagande; ils feront appel aux sentiments religieux de leurs adeptes pour les engager à se grouper autour de ce Mahdi, qui fait précisément partie d'une de leurs confréries.

Cette insurrection—qui se produira, *sans aucune doute*, aussitôt après une seconde victoire du Mahdi, dans tous les pays arabes placés sous la domination ottomane—tout en donnant une satisfaction à l'Angleterre dont le but est l'affaiblissement du prestige de l'Islam, ne laissera pas de l'alarmer aussi. Les intentions plus ou moins déguisées de l'Angleterre sont d'affaiblir graduellement la Turquie pour s'attribuer ensuite la plus grande partie de ses possessions.

La Grande-Bretagne nourrit le dessein de former un petit Khalafat à la Mecque, au profit de la famille de Beni-Awn, dont l'un des membres est actuellement le chérif de la Mecque, afin de pouvoir disposer à sa guise d'un moyen tout-puissant de domination sur tous les musulmans.

Une insurrection semblable à celle que je prévois serait d'autant plus préjudiciable aux interêts des Anglais qu'elle nécessiterait l'intervention des puissances européennes ayant des interêts serieux en Orient. L'Angleterre, dès lors, pourrait bien voir lui échapper la large part qu'elle convoite dans le dépècement de la proie ottomane. Il ne serait pas impossible qu'il se formât en Orient—par suite de certaines complications qui surgiraient peut-être en Europe et empêcheraient l'intervention des puissances interessées—un Khalifat assez important pour les Arabes. Ces deux eventualités ne sont pas moins funestes l'une que l'autre pour les Anglais.

Mais quoi! l'Angleterre espère-t-elle donc, par ses procédés habituels, c'est à dire par la ruse, la fourberie, par son addresse à s'introduire dans les pays, par le désir qu'elle manifeste hypocritement de rendre les populations heureuses, de leur assurer la securité et le bien-être, et, après avoir enraciné la haine dans les coeurs de tous les musulmans, en arrachant des mains de l'Islam le plus vaste et les plus riche royaume du monde, cet empire timorien-indien qui compte 250 millions d'âmes environ, espère-t-elle, dis-je étouffer la voix du Mahdi, la plus formidable de toutes les voix puisqu'elle dépasse en puissance la voix même de la guerre sainte, qui sort de toutes les bouches musulmanes!

Croit-elle pouvoir l'étouffer avant qu'elle se soit fait entendre dans toutes les parties de l'Orient, des monts Himalaya à Dawlaghir, du Nord jusqu'au Midi, s'adressant aux musulmans de l'Afghanistan, du Bélouchistan, du Sindh et des Indes et proclamant hautement la venue du Sauveur qu'attend tout enfant de l'Islam avec tant d'impatience: *El-Mahdi, El-Mahdi, El-Mahdi*!

Est-ce en abandonnant le Soudan au Mahdi, comme l'insinuent la plupart des journaux anglais, et en concluant la paix entre Mohamed-Ahmed et le gouvernement égyptien, dans l'unique but de s'emparer plus tard elle-même du Soudan (comme l'a dit, d'ailleurs, une partie de la presse française), est-ce ainsi que l'Angleterre espère reussir à faire taire cette voix terrible du Mahdi? Ce serait une idée absolument chimérique; car celui qui se lève sous un nom religieux, se déclarant prophète ou mahdi, ne s'arrête jamais dans son chemin, convaincu que s'il recule, la confiance que ses partisans ont en lui commencera par s'affaiblir et finira indubitablement par disparaître.

La devise d'un Mahdi ne peut donc être que celle-ci: Mourir, ou bien arriver au but qu'il s'est proposé.

Est-ce en recourant aux troupes françaises, démontrant, par là, sa faiblesse ignorée des Orientaux, que l'Angleterre compte étouffer la voix du Mahdi? En ce cas, elle désavouerait ainsi son passé, reviendrait à l'état de choses qu'elle a détruit, et, sans le vouloir, donnerait l'Egypte aux égyptiens. C'est ce que nous désirons, au risque de voir le malheureux Gladstone tomber du pouvoir.

L'Angleterre, désespérant de conclure la paix avec le Mahdi, de propose-t-elle d'amener des troupes indiennes musulmanes au Soudan? D'abord, est-ce possible? Comment le gouvernement anglais pourrait-il s'imaginer que des musulmans, pour le plaisir de consolider la puissance de leur ennemi héréditaire, de l'Anglais, soient capables d'entrer en guerre avec un homme qui paraît pour raffermir leur foi?

Ou bien croit-elle parvenir à tromper les Indiens dans cette affaire, comme elle les a trompés dans l'affaire d'Arabi, et leur faire croire qu'elle ne fait, cette fois encore, que venir en aide au sultan pour réprimer des rebelles? Les Indiens ont acquis la certitude, après ce qui s'est passé en Egypte, que l'Angleterre est

Appendix II

décidée à jouer, avec la Turquie, le même rôle qu'elle a joué avec la puissance timorienne.

Ou bien s'imagine-t-elle faire appel aux soldats de Siki et de Kourkou ? Ce dernier parti, outre qu'il aurait pour résultat d'aggraver, contre les Anglais, la haine des Indiens musulmans, qui ne verront pas sans peine et sans amertume les Indous aller en guerre contre leur sauveur (le Mahdi) pourrait avoir une autre conséquence non moins désastreuse pour les Anglais : celle de surexciter les populations musulmanes indiennes à tel point qu'elles profiteraient sans doute de l'absence d'une partie des troupes anglaises dans les Indes.

Le cheich Gemal-Ed-Din-El-Afghan.

4.

Le Mahdi (L'INTRANSIGEANT, *17 December, 1883*)

III

Pour se rendre un compte exact des inquiétudes que les victoires successives de Mohamed-Ahmed (le Mahdi) inspirent aux Anglais, habiles à dissimuler leurs pensées et leurs intentions, il est indispensable de connaître le situation de l'Angleterre dans les Indes, les sentiments des populations indiennes à son égard, et enfin les veritables proportions de sa force militaire dans ce pays.

Le nombre des soldats européens dont la Grande-Bretagne peut disposer ne dépasse pas 50,000. Ces 50,000 Anglais sont disséminés sur tous les points du territoire indien et jusqu'en Birmanie. L'Angleterre ne pourrait en aucune façon compter sur les soldats musulmans et indous, en cas d'insurrection, car il n'est pas une seule grande maison dans l'Indoustan qu'elle n'ait mutilée ou détruite, pas un coeur qu'elle n'ait froissé, ne faisant aucune distinction d'ailleurs entre les Musulmans et les Indous.

L'Angleterre a arraché à l'Islam l'immense royaume timorien, comme elle avait usurpé le gouvernment des Mirits, qui sont les plus vaillants et les plus nombreux des Indous. Elle a ravi le Sindh aux nababs, le Pengab aux rajahs de Sik. Elle a anéanti les nababs du Bengale sans épargner les royaumes de Mysore et d'Awed, qu'elle a dépeuplés par des massacres. Elle a, enfin, démembré les territoires des rajahs de Djeypour, de Djotpour et de Brouda, et s'en est attribué la plus grande partie.

Les rajahs et nababs, fort peu nombreux d'ailleurs, qui conservent encore leurs royaumes, ne sont point rassurés sur les futurs projets de l'Angleterre ; ils ignorent si celle-ci consentira à les laisser en possession de leurs biens, et s'attendent à se voir d'un jour à l'autre dépouillés du peu qui leur reste. Ils ne se font aucune illusion sur le sort que leur préparent les convoitises britanniques. Les Anglais sont persuadés qu'à la moindre insurrection qui éclaterait dans les Indes, tous les soldats indigènes, les Musulmans aussi bien que les Indous, feront cause commune avec les insurgés, se grouperont sous un même drapeau, et, appuyés par les rajahs et les nababs qui appréhendent d'être dépossédés de leurs biens, se révolteront contre leur dominateur, sans même chercher les causes de cette insurrection, sans prendre le temps de réfléchir au profit qu'ils en tireront et sans examiner à quel résultat ils pourront aboutir.

Mohamed-Ahmed (le Mahdi) ne paraît pas ignorer la véritable situation des Anglais dans les Indes et leurs intentions, plus ou moins déguisées, de mettre la main sur la Mecque ; il ne se dissimule pas que la première lutte sérieuse qu'il aura à soutenir sera contre les Anglais en Egypte. Aussi a-t-il envoyé des émissaires et des proclamations aux *savants* de la Mecque et particulièrement aux *savants* émigrants de l'Indoustan, d'Afghanistan et de Bockara, lesquels sont établis dans la Mecque.

Dans cette proclamation, dont le texte sera publié à la première occasion propice, le Mahdi invite les Musulmans à se lever pour raffermir la foi musulmane et pour l'aider à accomplir sa mission divine. Et si, à cette heure, ces divers *savants* ne se sont pas encore prononcés en faveur de Mohamed-Ahmed, je ne doute pas un instant, comme je l'ai déja dit, qu'à la nouvelle d'une autre victoire sérieuse du Mahdi, laquelle achèverait de les édifier sur son compte, ils ne se rangent tous de son côté.

L'homme est, par sa nature, porté à exagérer toutes les nouvelles qui lui viennent de loin ; de sorte que le chiffre *un* passant d'une bouche à une autre, et grossi par la rumeur publique, ne tarde pas à devenir le chiffre *mille ;* la colline finit par être regardée comme une montagne. C'est pourquoi, à l'annonce de la venue d'un mahdi, les coeurs de ceux qui attendent leur émancipation s'empliront de grandes promesses et déborderont de joie et d'espoir.

Le premier mouvement se produira vraisemblablement chez les cheichs de Tourouk (confréries) *El-Chichtia,* de la famille des Olran-Schah de Bélouchistan, *El-Kadiria* au Sindh, *El-Tackchindia* et *El-Kadiria* des monts de l'Afghanistan, sous le commandement

Appendix II

du fils de Ahoundsiouath, et chez les Ouahabünes El-Majahidines, en Afghanistan et en Bélouchistan, sous le commandement de leur émir Abdullah. Tous ceux-là seront renforcés par la société des Mirits, qui réside à Pouna et qui comptait, il y a un an, plus de 500,000 membres. Cette société attend, non sans impatience, une occasion pour agir.

Ces mouvements formidables auront inévitablement pour contre-coup, dans les Indes, un soulèvement général dont il serait extrêmement difficile aux Anglais d'avoir raison. En tout cas, ils n'en viendront certainement pas à bout comme de la dernière insurrection.

Une autre victoire sérieuse du Mahdi—laquelle passerait incontestablement, aux yeux des Mahométans, pour un second miracle—aurait pour conséquence fatale non seulement de provoquer une insurrection dans les pays de l'Islam soumis à la domination turque, ainsi que dans le Bélouchistan, l'Afghanistan, le Sindh, l'Indoustan, Bockara, Khoukand, Khiva—mais aussi d'amener des troubles à Tripoli, à Tunis, en Algérie et jusqu'au Maroc. Car tous les Musulmans attendent le Mahdi et considèrent son arrivée comme une nécessité absolue.

Le seul remède, suivant moi, pour faire disparaître le mal avant qu'il se développe dans tout le corps, ne consiste pas, comme le croient certains journaux anglais importants, dans l'abandon du Soudan et la conclusion de la paix entre le Mahdi et le gouvernement égyptien, mais bien dans l'intervention turque, ou encore dans l'association des Français avec les Anglais, en vue de prévenir un désastre.

Mais les Anglais sont très éloignés de consentir à une intervention française; ils ne s'y résigneront pas avant que le poignard musulman soit enfoncé jusqu'à la garde dans leur coeur, et le remède serait alors inéfficace. En effet, ils ne sont entrés en Egypte, seuls, et contrairement aux voeux des Français, que parce qu'ils ont vu ceux-ci s'établir à Tunis. Ils ont alors fort bien compris qu'il ne restait plus à la France, l'une des puissances militaires le plus formidables, pour arriver à s'emparer de la porte des Indes—je veux dire de l'Egypte—que d'acquérir la Tripolitaine, laquelle se trouve actuellement entre les mains débiles de la Turquie.

Pourquoi l'Angleterre ne veut-elle pas, en cette affaire, entendre parler d'une intervention turque? Est-ce parce qu'elle redoute la Turquie, ou bien parce qu'elle craint que cette puissance ne lui ferme le chemin des Indes? Je ne crois ni à l'une ni à l'autre de ces hypothèses. La Turquie, en effet, n'a-t-elle pas, quand elle était beaucoup plus forte qu'elle ne l'est aujourd'hui, et avant le creusement du canal de Suez, laissé les soldats anglais traverser l'Egypte pour aller combattre ses coreligionnaires, les Indiens musulmans, et les déposséder de leurs biens ? La raison de l'attitude de l'Angleterre ne peut donc être, à mon avis, que la haine vouée aux Musulmans par les Anglais, et surtout par M. Gladstone, protestant fervent et théologien émérite.

Si la France et l'Angleterre ne déploient pas toute leur énergie pour prévenir certaines éventualités, il résultera de l'action de l'Angleterre seule, dans cette grave question, des désastres considérables pour ces deux puissances.

Quant aux deux hommes qui ambitionnent le khédiviat d'Egypte, l'ex-khédive Ismail et Halim-pacha, lesquels profitent de l'occasion que leur fournit le Mahdi pour entrer dans les bonnes grâces de l'Angleterre, je me bornerai, pour le moment, et afin de ne pas fatiguer le lecteur, à parler de l'un d'eux le plus brièvement possible.

Sans doute l'élévation de Halim-pacha au trône khédivial causerait un plaisir extrême à tous ceux qui souhaitent l'agrandissement et la consolidation de la puissance ottomane. Halim est, en effet, l'un des courtisans du sultan ; il lui promet sans cesse de placer le gouvernement du Caire sous la dépendance absolue du Divan de Constantinople, comme sont les vilayets de Syrie, d'Alep, etc., etc. Mais Halim n'a point de parti dans la vallée du Nil, il n'y est que fort peu connu, et le peu de gens qui le connaissent le considèrent comme un athée.

On concevra aisément, qu'un homme taxé d'impiété par les égyptiens, qui sont profondément religieux, ne saurait tenir tête à Mohamed-Ahmed, qui apparaît aux populations avec le prestige de son titre religiux de *Mahdi*. Il est vrai qu'Arabi-pacha a prononcé le nom d'Halim-pacha ; il a même déclaré qu'il l'acceptait pour khédive ; mais il ne faut pas en conclure qu'il était le partisan d'Halim ou que celui-ci avait un parti en Egypte.

C'est seulement lorsqu'Arabi fut mis au pied du mur et sommé de se prononcer pour l'un des prétendants au trône khédivial, qu'il s'est, dans l'intention de raffermir sa situation en Egypte, déclaré en faveur d'Halim.

Quant à l'ex-khedive Ismail, je lui consacrerai un article spécial,[193] où je mettrai en parallèle les conséquences fâcheuses et les bons résultats que pourrait avoir sa restauration au khédiviat. Le cheich Gemal-Ed-Din-El-Afghan.

Appendix III

Letter from Afghani to Sir Philip Currie enclosed with despatch no. 923 from Constantinople, 12 December, 1895, F.O. 60/594.

Constantinople le 19 nov^{re}

Excellence!
Vous représentez un gouvernement qui tient de si haut l'Etendard de la civilisation et qui répand partout les bienfaits de l'humanité. Votre action se ressent surtout en Orient, pays où Chrétiens ainsi que Musulmans, ont toujours été en butte à la torture et à la tyrannie. Vous avez toujours été le protecteur zélé des faibles qui gémissent sous le joug des ambitions injustes et barbares. Bien convaincu de votre haut sentiment, permettez-moi de porter à votre connaissance ce qui suit. Je suis Afghan (Cabul) et je dépend de l'Angleterre. J'ai passé une grande partie de ma vie en Orient dans le seul but de déraciner le fanatisme, la plus fâcheuse maladie de ce pays, réformer la société et y établir les bienfaits de la tolérance. Voilà ce que je m'y suis proposé. J'ai aussi séjourné assez longtemps dans les principales capitales de l'Europe où j'ai eu l'occasion d'être dans la société des plus grands personnages, de hommes d'Etat, des amis de la Presse et des grands Savants. Je me trouvais à Londres lorsque j'ai reçu l'invitation de S.M.I. le Sultan et voilà comment je me suis trouvé son hôte. Je ne croyais pas que pareille invitation aurait jamais pu porter préjudice, car en venant à Constantinople, je me suis trouvé en face de folles intrigues et fourberies de toutes sortes, plongé dans une suite de calomnies absurdes et insignifiantes. Sur quoi j'ai à plusieurs reprises demandé mon congé ce qui m'a été refusé. Durant ces derniers événements (c.a.d. la question d'Arménie) qui ont encore obscurci la situation, en multipliant les faux mensonges et les calomnies absurdes S.M.I. qui semble flotter au milieu de son entourage s'est laissé influencer par certains de sa cour de sorte qu'un grand nombre d'innocents ont été sans cause ni raison expulsés etc. ...

Etant venu ici comme hôte, je n'ai été naturellement que le simple spectateur de toutes ces affaires.

S.M.I. toujours guidé par des vagues soupçons suggérés par son entourage, fit assiéger ma maison par la police, sans que je puis encore m'en expliquer la cause, et ce qui est plus pénible, c'est que je me trouve dans une situation douteuse, ne sachant quel sera l'effet de ces impressions.

Toujours est-il que je me trouve très gêné. Notez, Excellence, que, quoique étranger à ce pays et encore étant venu de Londres comme hôte de S.M.I. et à son invitation le fait est que je n'ai pas eu un moment de tranquillité.

Vous pouvez donc conclure, Excellence, combien de milliers de pauvres personnes—qui par malheur se trouvent sous les griffes des bourreaux sans conscience—crient au secours! Des milliers de Mussulmans et Chrétiens, exclament du fond de leur coeur Sauvez-nous! Sauvez-nous! car comme toujours c'est le hasard qui décide des choses ici et non pas la raison et la justice.

Je viens donc au nom de l'humanité attirer votre attention sur cet état de choses, et vous prier de prendre en considération ma démarche.

Veuillez agréer etc.

(S.) Djemalledin El Husseini El Afghani.

Notes

[1] *The Persian Revolution of 1905–1909*, Cambridge 1910, p. xii. Pp. xi–xx of this work show that Browne had evolved and adopted a reasoned, systematic doctrine of nationalism.
[2] *Modern Egypt*, Vol. II, p. 180.
[3] *Comparative Studies in Society and History*, Vol. IV, 1962, pp. 265–95.
[4] Berkeley 1962.
[5] *Op. cit.*, pp. 6 ff and 18–19.
[6] There had been an earlier essay by Max Horten, "Muhammad Abduh, Sein Leben und sein theologisch-philosophische Gedankenwelt" in *Beiträge zur Kenntnis des Orients*, Vol. XIII and XIV, Halle 1916 and 1917.
[7] See Haim, *op. cit.*, pp. 25–28.
[8] Abd al-Qadir al-Maghribi, *al-Bayyinat*, Vol. I, Cairo 1926, pp. 150–1. What Antonius did for Kawakibi others now seem intent on doing for a writer even more obscure, the Egyptian Marsafi, author of a tract only the reading of which can indicate its utter insignificance. Yet Marsafi is made into a precursor and his work into a turning-point. See J. Ahmed, *The Intellectual Origins of Egyptian Nationalism*, 1960; and I. Abu Loghd, *The Arab Rediscovery of Europe*, Princeton 1963.
[9] H. A. R. Gibb, *Modern Trends in Islam*, Chicago 1947, p. 28.
[10] *The Times*, 8 September 1879, p. 6, col. 5, despatch "From a Correspondent", Cairo, 30 August.
[11] Despatch Secret No. 424, Cairo, 23 October, 1886, F.O. 60/594, Public Record Office, London.
[12] Despatch No. 923 from Sir P. Currie, Constantinople, 12 December 1895, F.O. 60/594.
[13] *Tarikh al-ustadh al-imam*, Vol. I, Cairo 1931, pp. 890 and 934.
[14] One example is mentioned in E. Kedourie, *England and the Middle East*, London 1956, p. 115.
[15] Rashid Rida to Antonius, 10 January 1935; see E. Kedourie, "Egypt and the Caliphate", *Journal of the Royal Asiatic Society*, October 1963, p. 229.
[16] "Afghani in Afghanistan" in *Middle Eastern Studies*, Vol. I, no. 4.
[17] See N. Berkes, *The Development of Secularism in Turkey*, Montreal, 1964. Professor Berkes has given a convincing account of the circumstances which led to Afghani giving his lecture and of the attacks which followed.
[18] Abd al-Qadir Maghribi, *Jamal al-Din al Afghani*, Cairo 1948, states, p. 30, that he has in his possession a manuscript refutation of Afghani's views written by his father who was then in Istanbul, '*Ayn al-sawab fi'l radd 'ala man qal in'al-risala wa'l-nubuwwa san'atan tunalan bi'l-iktisab*, i.e., *The most correct refutation of him who says that the apostolate and prophethood are crafts which can be acquired [by effort]*. Professor Berkes also examines another refutation of Afghani written by the *'alim*, Khalil Fauzi, entitled *al-Suyuf al-qawati'* (*The Cutting Swords*), *op. cit.*, pp. 185–6.
[19] Abd al-Rahman Badawi, *Min tarikh al-ilhad fi'l-Islam* (*Chapters in the History of Atheism in Islam*), Cairo, 1945, p. 198 ff.
[20] Adib Ishaq, *al-Durar*, ed. Jirjis Mikha'il Nahhas, Alexandria 1886, p. 40. The detail occurs in a biographical notice of Afghani which Rashid Rida copied in his *Tarikh*, with this particular detail, however, omitted.

[21] Salim Rufa'il Jirjis al-'Anhuri, *Sihr Harut* (*Harut's Magic*), Damascus 1885, pp. 178–9. 'Anhuri was Adib Ishaq's contemporary and friend and came to Egypt in 1878.
[22] Rashid Rida, *Tarikh*, vol. I, p. 31.
[23] 'Anhuri, *op. cit.*, pp. 178–9.
[24] F.O. 60/594.
[25] Rashid Rida, *Tarikh*, I, p. 72.
[26] Muhammad al Makhzumi, *Khatirat Jamal al-Din al-Afghani* (*Reminiscences of Jamal al-Din* . . .), Beirut 1931, pp. 110–11.
[27] Shakib Arslan in a note on Afghani in L. Stoddard, *Hadir al-'alam al-islami* (*The Muslim World To-Day*) Cairo 1925, Vol. I, pp. 199–209. The quotations above are at p. 207.
[28] Muhammad Salam Madkur, *Jamal al-Din al-Afghani*, Cairo 1937, p. 129.
[29] The *Risala* was included in the first edition of Vol. II of Rashid Rida, *Tarikh*, published in 1908, but was omitted from the second edition published in 1926; it would seem that it was separately reprinted in Cairo in 1925. See 'Uthman Amin, *Ra'id al-fikr al-misri*, Cairo, 1955, p. 261. I have not been able to see the text of the *Risala*, but B. Michel and Moustapha Abdel Razik summarise its contents and quote extensively from its preface in the introduction to their *Rissalat al Tawhid: Exposé de la Religion Musulmane* . . . , Paris 1925. The summary and quotation above are taken from p. xxi.
[30] There seems to have been another work by 'Abduh which is now lost, with the revealing title, *Wahdat al-wujud, The Unity of Existence;* see 'Uthman Amin, *op. cit.*, p. 264.
[31] *Op. cit.*, p. xx.
[32] The commentary was first published in Cairo in 1905; see 'Uthman Amin, *op. cit.*, p. 261. There is a new edition with a very critical introduction by Sulaiman Dunia, *al-Shaikh Muhammad 'Abduh bain al-falasifa wa'l-kalamiyyin*, 2 vols., Cairo, 1958. Dunia is unique in his criticisms.
[33] *Al-Manar*, Vol. XXIII (1922), p. 527.
[34] A. M. Broadley, *How we defended Arabi and his friends*, London 1884, p. 227.
[35] E. G. Browne, *A year among the Persians*, 1926 ed., p. 14.
[36] 'Uthman Amin, *op. cit.*, p. 32.
[37] W. S. Blunt, *Gordon at Khartoum*, London 1911, p. 274.
[38] *Rissalat al-tawhid*, pp. 71–2 of the French translation cited above; on Afghani's utilitarianism see Haim, *op. cit.*, pp. 9–13.
[39] *Rissalat al-tawhid*, French translation, pp. 33–4.
[40] *al-Manar*, Cairo, Vol. I [1315 (1898)], 2nd ed. 1327, p. 465.
[41] See the third Arabic ed. of the *Risala*, edited by Rashid Rida, Cairo 1337, p. 33 f.1.
[42] "Religion and irreligion . . . ", *loc. cit.*
[43] Haim, *op. cit.*, p. 11.
[44] Mustafa Abd al-Raziq, *Muhammad 'Abduh*, Cairo, 1946, pp. 74–5. The same passage occurs in Mustafa Abd al-Raziq's lecture reported in *al-Manar*, vol. XXIII, mentioned above, but there Mustafa Abd al-Raziq adds, p. 526, the interesting observation that when Abduh wrote his commentary on Iji's '*Aqa'id* he had become a complete votary of Matatia's café.
[45] Maghribi, *op. cit.*, pp. 48–9.

Notes

[46] Makhzumi, *op. cit.*, p. 82, also pp. 213 ff; Haim, *op. cit.*, p. 18.
[47] Afghani's comment on Renan's lecture is printed by A–M. Goichon in the translation of Afghani's treatise *Réfutation des Matérialistes*, Paris 1942; 'Abduh's views on science and religion are found in his treatise *al-Islam wa'l-nasraniyya (Islam and Christianity* . . .), Cairo 1902.
[48] 'Abbas Mahmud al-'Aqqad, *Rijāl 'araftuhum (Men I have known)*, Cairo 1963, pp. 183–4.
[49] Muhammad Ahmad Khalafallah, *Abdullah al-Nadim wa mudhakkiratuhu al-siyasiyya (A.N. and his Political Memoirs)* Cairo 1956, p. 52.
[50] Rashid Rida, *Tarikh I*, p. 39.
[51] *Op. cit.*, pp. 43 and 50. 'Anhuri's account of Afghani's philosophical views is copied in Rashid Rida's *Tarikh* from *Sihr Harut* but Rashid Rida gives little else of 'Anhuri's most interesting notice.
[52] *Op. cit.*, p. 32.
[53] Letter from Syed Hussein, 20 June 1883, to Mr. Cordery, Resident at Hyderabad, enclosed with a letter from the Secretary of the Government of India to the Secretary, Political and Secret Department, India Office, 13 July 1883, F.O. 60/594.
[54] Ahmad Shukri and 'Ali Lutfi, *Siham al-tadmir fi sudur ashab al-masamir (The arrows of destruction in the hearts of the authors of al-masamir)* Cairo [?], n.d., p. 2. The pamphlet is remarkably polite and moderate in tone.
[55] 'Anhuri, *op. cit.*, pp. 179 & 185.
[56] Maghribi, *op. cit.*, pp. 39–40.
[57] The fullest account in English of al-Nadim and his writings is found in London University Ph.D. thesis, 1959, *Abdallah Nadim*, by Ali al-Hadidi.
[58] See *al-Durar* (a collection of his articles) edited by his brother Awni Ishaq, Beirut 1909, pp. 189 and 246; also Louis Cheikho, *al-Adab al-'arabiyya fi'l qarn al-tasi' 'ashar (Arabic Literature in the nineteenth century)* 2nd ed., Beirut 1926,Vol. II, p. 133.
[59] Auni Ishaq in the introduction to *al-Durar*, p. 10; Cheikho *op. cit.*, p. 133.
[60] For Sanua's biography see Ibrahim 'Abduh, *Abu Naddara*, Cairo 1953; the first leading article is quoted p. 42 and Sanua's account of his break with Isma'il, p. 38; see also, *ibid.*, *A'lam al-sahafa al-'arabiyya (The Masters of Arabic Journalism)* Cairo, 1944, p. 70.
[61] *Loc. cit.*, p. 276. On Malkam Khan's quarrel with the Shah see a series of telegrams between the Foreign Office, London, and the Minister in Tehran in November-December 1889, in F.O. 60/504. See also W. S. Blunt, *Secret History of the British Occupation of Egypt*, 1907, p. 83.
[62] See Filib de Tarrazi, *Tarikh al-sahafa al-'arabiyya (History of Arab Journalism*, Vol. II, Beirut 1913, pp. 73 ff and 251–2.
[63] Blunt, *op. cit.*, pp. 86–7. On Sabunji's career see further Blunt, *op. cit.*, p. 299 f.1 and the biographical notice in Jurji Zaidan, *Tarajim mashahir al-sharq (Biographies of celebrated easterners)*, 3rd ed., Cairo 1922.
[64] F.O. 78/3003, Despatch Political No. 498 from Frank C. Lascelles, Cairo, 30 August, 1879.
[65] Keddie, *loc. cit.*, Cheikho, *op. cit.*, p. 133; Ibrahim Abduh, *op. cit.*, p. 59.
[66] Jurji Zaidan, *Tarikh al-masuniyya al-'am (General History of Freemasonry)*, 2nd ed., Cairo 1921, p. 155.

[67] R. F. Gould, *History of Freemasonry*, ed. Rev. Herbert Poole, London, 1951, Vol. III, pp. 33–4. Mildred J. Headings, *French Freemasonry under the Third Republic*, p. 41, states that Comte de Saint-Simon was a mason.

[68] Headings, *op. cit.*, p. 35; Zaydan, *op. cit.*, p. 153; Gaston Martin, *Manuel d'Histoire de la Franc-Maçonnerie Française*, Paris 1929, p. 225.

[69] Makhzumi, *op. cit.*, pp. 41–44; Rashid Rida, *Tarikh*, Vol. 1, pp. 40–41, 'Abduh's biographical notice. Afghani used to complain that the British sought to impose their authority in the Lodge; one writer, M. Sabry, *La Genèse de l'Esprit National Egyptien (1863–1882)*, Paris 1924, p. 142, mentions Ralph Borg, a British Vice-Consul at Cairo, as having been prominent in Egyptian masonry at this time; Sabry mentions no sources, and his account seems, in general, confused, but it may be that Borg adopted a line opposed to Afghani's in the Grand Architect controversy, which would explain Afghani's subsequent attacks. Borg would also, in this case, have given Lascelles his information about Afghani's explusion. Borg was quite knowledgeable about Egyptian society and politics, as may be seen from his despatches during this period.

[70] 'Abduh's letter to Afghani from Beirut, previously mentioned. Rashid Rida's version lacks this particular detail which is found in the letter as reproduced in *Documents*, plates 134–7.

[71] Maghribi, *op. cit.*, p. 74, recording a conversation of Afghani's during his last period in Istanbul.

[72] Reproduced in *Documents*, plate 40.

[73] Sabry, *op. cit.*, p. 172.

[74] *Documents*, plate 32.

[75] Rashid Rida, *Tarikh I*, pp. 40–1; Makhzumi, *op. cit.*, p. 41.

[76] *Al-Manar*, Vol. VIII, 1905, pp. 402–4. 'Abduh himself was very discreet in what he told Blunt about his masonic activities; Blunt, *op. cit.*, p. 491.

[77] Blunt, *op. cit.*, pp. 83–4.

[78] A. K. S. Lambton, "Secret Societies and the Persian Revolution", *St. Antony's Papers IV*, London 1958, p. 48. See also A. de Gobineau, *Les religions et les philosophies dans l'Asie centrale*, 2nd ed., Paris 1866, pp. 305–7.

[79] See Rashid Rida, *Tarikh I*, p. 992, who quotes an article by Mehmet 'Akif, a Tartar, in an Orenburg newspaper to the effect that it was common to accuse reformers in Arabic of Wahabism, in Turkey of Freemasonry and in Persia of Babism.

[80] Gould, *op. cit.*, pp. 33–4.

[81] On Jean Meslier see, e.g., Ira O. Wade, *The Clandestine Organisation and Diffusion of Philosophic Ideas in France from 1700 to 1750*, Princeton, 1938.

[82] 'Anhuri, *op. cit.*, pp. 180–1.

[83] *Modern Egypt*, Vol. I, London 1908, p. 45.

[84] F.O. 78/2998, despatch no. 21 Political, Most Secret and Confidential from Vivian, Cairo, 11 January 1879.

[85] On Isma'il's role see Cromer, *op. cit.*, Vol. I, pp. 79–81, and Blunt, *Secret History* . . . , pp. 46–8.

[86] F.O. 78/3000, despatches from F. C. Lascelles, Cairo, Political no. 175 of 1 April 1879, no. 180 of 4 April, no. 203 of 10 April and no. 242 of 22 April.

[87] Haim, *op. cit.*, p. 8.

[88] Blunt, *Secret history* . . . , p. 489.

Notes 93

[89] Rashid Rida, *Tarikh I*, p. 41; F.O. 78/3001, despatch from Vivian, Political no. 311, Cairo, 24 May, 1879. Ahmed Abdel-Rehim Mustafa, *The Domestic and Foreign Affairs of Egypt from 1876 to 1882*, Ph.D. thesis, London University, 1955, examines the evidence of the French archives and shows France's consistent hostility to Isma'il.

[90] The addresses are enclosed with despatch Political no. 189 of 7 April, 1879 from Lascelles, Cairo, in F.O. 78/3000.

[91] *Khedives and Pashas*, 1884, "Cherif Pasha", pp. 163–184.

[92] Baron des Michels, *Souvenirs de Carrière (1855–1886)*, Paris 1901, p. 122.

[93] F.O. 78/3003, despatches from Lascelles, Cairo, nos. 474 of 19 August, 1879; 477 of 21 August; and 515 of 21 September.

[94] *Documents*, plates 34–37. The *Documents* reproduce the drafts of two other letters written at the same time, plates 32 and 33, which give no indication of the recipient; it appears, however, from Mahmud Qasim, *Jamal al-Din al-Afghani*, Cairo, n.d., p. 218 that the letter on plate 33 was sent to Abdullah Fikri on whom see article by J. Jomier in the *Encyclopaedia of Islam*, 2nd ed.

[95] F.O. 78/3003, despatch Political no. 498 of 30 August, 1879, cited above.

[96] F.O. 407/71 (confidential print), no. 9, Intelligence Dept., War Office to Foreign Office, 19 July, 1887.

[97] *Documents*, plates 106–117.

[98] 'Anhuri, *op. cit.*, p. 182.

[99] The text of the official announcement as published in al-Ahram of 28 August, 1879, is reproduced in Muhammad Subaih, *Muhammad 'Abduh*, Cairo 1944, pp. 55–7.

[100] *Documents*, plate 32.

[101] Blunt, *Secret history* . . . , p. 493.

[102] An official in the Board of Education, friend of Abdullah Fikri mentioned above.

[103] Rashid Rida, *Tarikh I*, *loc. cit.*

[104] Rashid Rida, *Tarikh I*, pp. 175 and 976 ff.

[105] J. Ninet, "Origin of the National Party in Egypt", *Nineteenth Century*, January 1883, pp. 131–2.

[106] In Rashid Rida's text the names of Adib Ishaq and the others who abandoned Afghani were suppressed and replaced by intitials. From the text in the *Documents*, it appears that those who roused 'Abduh's ire were Adib Ishaq, Salim al-Naqqash, Sa'id al-Bustani, all Syrian Christian journalists, and the Egyptian Ibrahim al-Halbawi.

[107] Sabry, *op. cit.*, p. 173; Rashid Rida, *Tarikh I*, p. 186; Abd al-Latif Hamza, *Adab al-maqala al-suhufiyya fi-misr*, Vol. II, Cairo, 1950, pp. 13 ff.

[108] Rashid Rida, *Tarikh I*, p. 186; Blunt, *Secret history* . . . , p. 252.

[109] Blunt, *Secret History* . . . , p. 196.

[110] Rashid Rida, *Tarikh I*, *loc. cit.*, as amplified by *Documents*, plates 134–7.

[111] Rashid Rida, *Tarikh I*, pp. 183–5. No. 7 of *al-Urwa al-wuthqa* (1 May, 1884), carries an article in praise of Riad, *Riad Pasha wa'l-siyasa al-ingiliziyya* (Riad Pasha and English Policy). This may have been one reason why the Indian C.I.D., as has been said above, suspected that Riad was financing Afghani in Paris. Makhzumi, *op. cit.*, records, pp. 402–4, a long eulogy which Afghani made of Riad in his last Istanbul period.

[112] Rashid Rida, *Tarikh I, loc. cit.*, as amplified by text in *Documents*.
[113] Broadley, *op. cit.*, p. 229.
[114] Broadley, *op. cit.*, p. 227; on his political activities during the 'Urabi revolution, see Blunt, *Secret History* . . . , *passim*.
[115] See Edward Malet, *Egypt 1879–1883*, 1909, pp. 346 ff. for the attempt of the powers on May 21–22, 1882, to exile 'Urabi and his principal supporters.
[116] Headings, *op. cit.*, p. 25 f.23, quoting Samuel Pritchard, *Masonry Dissected*, New York, 1857. 'Abduh's interrogatory is found in Salim Khalil al-Naqqash, *Misr li'l-misriyyin*, Vol. VII, Alexandria 1884, pp. 164–5; Ya 'qub Sami's is on p. 102.
[117] F.O. 60/594, letter from Syed Hussein previously cited; memorandum by the General Superintendent Thagi and Dakaiti Dept., previously cited.
[118] Adib Ishaq's long poem praising Sharif and attacking 'Urabi in Naqqash *op. cit.*, Vol. V, pp. 242–5.
[119] See his numerous newspapers which do not, however, bear up his general reputation as a satirist, being mostly quite dull; also Ibrahim 'Abduh, *op. cit.*, p. 71 and A. Lemaitre, *Abou Neddara à Stamboul*, Paris 1892. For Sanua's support of Halim see Jacob M. Landau, *Parliaments and Parties in Egypt*, Tel-Aviv 1953, p. 95.
[120] Blunt, *Secret history* . . . , p. 299 f.1. Sabunji's *Diwan*, Cairo 1905, contains many poems in praise of Abdul Hamid.
[121] Baring's despatch No. 252 of June 9, 1889, F.O. 78/4241, where he states that it was on his suggestion that the Khedive pardoned 'Abduh and restored him to his religious title and seniority as a public official.
[122] Cromer's despatch no. 108, Cairo, 13 June, 1899, F.O. 78/5023.
[123] Cutting of the Gazette enclosed with Cromer's despatch no. 95 of 18 May, F.O. 78/5023.
[124] Cromer to Salisbury, Cairo 19 May, 1899, *Cromer Papers*, F.O. 633, vol. VI, p. 309.
[125] Draft report for 1899 in F.O. 78/5086.
[126] Despatch no. 105 of 6 June, 1899, in F.O. 78/5023.
[127] *al-Urwa al-wuthqa*, no. 7 (1 May, 1884).
[128] F.O. 60/594, despatch from Lord Lyons, Paris, 19 June, 1883, no. 393, Secret; letter from the Préfet de Police, Paris, 6 July, 1883.
[129] On Khalil Ghanim see E. E. Ramsaur Jr., *The Young Turks*, Princeton 1957, and R. Devereux, *The First Ottoman Constitutional Period*, Baltimore 1963.
[130] *E.g.* nos. 67 and 68 (15 and 22 February, 1883) an article on *al-sharq wa'l-sharqiyyin* (The East and the Easterners); no. 77 (26 April, 1883) an article on *manafi' al wifaq wa-madar al-shiqaq* (Benefits of Union and Harm of Disunion); see also below.
[131] Ernest Renan in *Journal des Débats*, 19 May, 1883; this article is reprinted as an Appendix to Renan's lecture, "L'Islamisme et la science" in his *Discours et Conférences*, Paris, 1887, pp. 402–409.
[132] I have not myself been able to see the issue of *La Justice* in which the French version appeared, but *al-Basir* printed what it stated to be the Arabic original in its issues nos. 74 and 75 of 5 and 12 April, 1883. *Al-Basir* stated that extracts from this article had appeared in the *Standard*, the *Daily Telegraph*, the *Globe*, the *Daily News* and the *Neue Freie Presse*.

Notes

[133] Renan's lecture itself had appeared in the *Journal des Débats* of 29 March, 1883.
[134] *Al Basir*, nos. 77 and 78 (26 April and 3 May, 1883).
[135] E. Renan, *op. cit.*, pp. 402–3. In a biographical notice prefixed to an edition of *al-'Urwa al-wuthqa* published in Beirut in 1933, Mustafa Abd al-Raziq translates this passage with no comment.
[136] Plates 138–140.
[137] *Al-Basir*, which I was able to consult only up to no. 83 (7 June 1883), has neither the text of Renan's lecture nor Afghani's comment. It in fact stated that it would not publish Renan's lecture since such a subject was not within its scope; no. 77 (26 April).
[138] *al-Manar*, vol. XXIV (1923) p. 311. Rashid Rida is here summarising the lecture. The text of the lecture was published in *al-Siyyasa* of 21 and 22 March, 1923; see Mahmud abu Rayya, *Jamal al-Din al-Afghani*, Cairo 1961, pp. 40 ff. I have not been able to consult *al-Siyyasa* for these dates.
[139] *al-Manar*, XXIV, p. 315.
[140] Shakib Arslan, *al-Sayyid Rashid Rida*, Damascus, 1937, p. 370.
[141] Ahmad al-Sharabasi, *Amir al-bayan Shakib Arslan* vol. II, Cairo 1963, pp. 653 ff, where the letter from Shakib Arslan to Rashid Rida is printed.
[142] *Les aventures de ma vie*, vol. IV, Paris 1897, pp. 345 ff.
[143] J. Ohrwalder, *Ten Years Captivity in the Mahdi's Camp, 1882–1892*, 10th ed,. 1893, p. 195. See also R. C. Slatin, *Fire and sword in the Sudan*, 1896, pp. 306 ff.
[144] *Al-Basir*, no. 78 (3 May 1883) published an Arabic summary of this article.
[145] I. Goldziher, *Le dogme et la loi de l'Islam*, Paris 1920, pp. 185–6.
[146] See article "Mahdi" by D. B. MacDonald in *Encyclopaedia of Islam*, article "Mahdi" by D. S. Margoliouth in *Hastings' Encyclopaedia of Religion and Ethics*, and C. Snouck Hurgronje, *Mohammedanism*, New York 1916, p. 107.
[147] See examples of his epistles and manifestos in Na'um Shuqair, *Tarikh al-Sudan al-hadith*, Cairo 1903, Pt. III, pp. 122 ff., and in Sa'd Muhammad Hasan, *Al-mahdiyya fi'l-islam*, Cairo 1953, pp. 229 ff. The archives dept. of the Sudan Government has recently published the collection of his epistles, *Kitab al-indharat* (The Book of Admonitions) as vol. II of *Manshurat al-mahdi*, Khartoum 1963. I am grateful to Professor P. M. Holt for drawing my attention to this work.
[148] I. Goldziher, *op. cit.*, p. 246.
[149] The saying is found, for instance, in the treatise by the Shafi'ite Shihab al-Din Ahmad ibn Hajar al-Haitami (d. 974/1565) entitled *al-Sawa'iq al-muhriqa fi'l-radd 'ala ahl al-bida' wa'l-zandaqa*, Cairo ed., 1956, (ed. Abd al-Wahhab Abd al-Latif), p. 164.
[150] See the text of two *fatwas* by Sudanese divines in Shuqair, *op. cit.*, pp. 375–91. See also J. Darmsteter, *Le Mahdi*, Paris 1885, p. 89. Darmsteter's book, authoritative, concise and witty, is written in a style which our more solemn orientalists have for the most part forsaken.
[151] Shuqair, *op. cit.*, p. 374.
[152] Mouradja d'Ohsson, *Tableau Général de l'Empire Ottoman*, Paris 1788, Vol. 1 (which is a translation of Halabi's treatise), p. 266.

153 The open letter is published in *al-Basir*, no. 66 (8 February 1883) and reprinted in *al-Manar*, Vol. XXVI (1925), pp. 44–47.
154 *Documents*, plates 101–105.
155 *Al-Urwa al-wuthqa*, Beirut 1933 ed., pp. 321, 324, 329–30 and 453–7.
156 W. S. Blunt, *Gordon at Khartoum*, London 1911, p. 492.
157 Blunt, *Gordon at Khartoum*, p. 500, diary entry for 2 November, 1885.
158 F.O. 60/594, despatch from Baring, Cairo, 23 October, 1886, Secret no. 424.
159 Keddie, "Afghani in Afghanistan", *loc. cit.*
160 F.O. 60/594, despatch from Morier, St. Petersburg 27 August, 1887, no. 299, reporting conversation with the Ottoman Ambassador; Blunt, *Gordon in Khartoum*, p. 501.
161 F.O. 60/594, despatch from Morier, St. Petersburg, 20 July, 1887, no. 253 Secret, enclosing translation of the article. Another translation made in the War Office is found in F.O. 407/71 as quoted above. It is interesting that the War Office translator thought it worth drawing attention to this article only because "this person's name has been mixed up with the proceedings of Dhuleep Singh".
162 Khushwant Singh, *The Fall of the Kingdom of the Punjab*, Calcutta 1962; material in "H" Books, Political and Secret Library, India Office Records, London.
163 India Office, Political and Secret Dept., Memorandum D83, *Affairs of the Maharajah Duleep Singh*, 31 December, 1888.
164 Memorandum D83 cited above, also despatch from Baring, no. 157 Secret, Cairo 12 April 1888, F.O. 78/4145.
165 F.O. 60/594, despatch from Morier, 27 August, 1887, no. 299, cited above.
166 F.O. 60/594, memorandum of the Thagi and Dakaiti Dept., 1896, cited above.
167 F.O. 60/594 despatch from Morier St. Petersburg, 27 April, 1892.
168 F.O. 60/594, telegram from Sir H. D. Wolff, 21 December, 1889.
169 Sir Henry Drummond Wolff, *Rambling Recollections*, Vol. II, 1908, pp. 329–30.
170 F.O. 60/502, despatch from Wolff, Teheran, 20 December, 1889, no. 241, enclosing memorandum by Mr. Churchill, Oriental Secretary, 18 December.
171 F.O. 60/594, despatch from Morier, St. Petersburg, 7 February, 1890, no. 40 Secret.
172 F.O. 60/594, despatch from Kennedy, Teheran, 12 January, 1891, no. 11.
173 F.O. 60/509, despatch no. 71, secret and confidential from Wolff, Teheran, 3 March, 1890, reporting that an anonymous letter denouncing Amin al-Sultan to the Shah was believed to be inspired by, among others, Amin al-Daulah and Malkam Khan.
174 F.O. 60/509, despatch no. 28 from Wolff, Teheran, 1 February, 1890, enclosing translation of an attack on Amin al-Sultan, appearing in the Moscow *Vedomosti*.
175 Browne, *op. cit.*, p. 10.
176 Browne, *op. cit.*, p. 31.
177 The Arabic text of these proclamations is found in F.O. 60/594.
178 F.O. 60/594, F.O. Memorandum, 17 December, 1895.
179 The *Documents*, plates 216 & 217, reproduce two letters from Abu'l Huda al-Sayyadi, dated Rajab 1309, pressing Afghani to settle in Istanbul and devote himself to the defence of the Caliphate.

[180] Keddie, *loc. cit.* 1962, appendix, translation of the preface to the Babi book, *Hasht Behesht*, pp. 292 ff.
[181] Browne, *op. cit.*, pp. 83 and 92.
[182] F.O. 78/4484, despatch, no. 596 confidential, from Sir A. Nicolson, Constantinople, 22 December, 1893. Sir Arthur Nicolson reported that Afghani's collaborator in this scheme was Abdullah al-Nadim.
[183] F.O. 60/594.
[184] Shakib Arslan, *loc. cit.*, in L. Stoddard, *op. cit.*, vol. I, p. 204. *La Jeune Turquie*, Paris (edited by Khalil Ghanim) in its no. of 27 December, 1895, quoted a report in the Cairo press that Afghani had had his pension cut off by the Sultan and had protested to the Ambassadors of the Great Powers, "who replied, most of them with all the respect due to his position."
[185] I am indebted to Mr. A. Qudsi-Zadeh for details of Crane's quest.
[186] *Tarikh*, I, p. 86.
[187] *al-Manar*, vol. xi, 1908, pp. 103–4.
[188] *al-Manar*, *loc. cit.*, pp. 188–9 and 197.
[189] For the Catholics see R. R. Palmer, *Catholics and Unbelievers* . . . , Princeton 1939; for the Jews, the forthcoming work by Mr. E. Marmorstein.
[190] W. S. Blunt, *My Diaries*, 1932 ed., pp. 276 and 289.
[191] Al-Tabari is no doubt meant.
[192] *Sic*. I cannot identify this reference.
[193] I have not been able to trace such an article in the files of *L'Intransigeant*.

Printed in the United Kingdom
by Lightning Source UK Ltd.
104593UKS00001BB/6